CHURCH UNITY AND THE PAPAL OFFICE

Church Unity and the Papal Office

An Ecumenical Dialogue
on John Paul II's Encyclical
Ut Unum Sint
(That All May Be One)

• •

Edited by

Carl E. Braaten *and* Robert W. Jenson

WILLIAM B. EERDMANS PUBLISHING COMPANY
GRAND RAPIDS, MICHIGAN / CAMBRIDGE, U.K.

© 2001 Wm. B. Eerdmans Publishing Co.
255 Jefferson Ave. S.E., Grand Rapids, Michigan 49503 /
P.O. Box 163, Cambridge CB3 9PU U.K.

Printed in the United States of America

05 04 03 02 01   7 6 5 4 3 2 1

Library of Congress Cataloging-in-Publication Data

Church unity and the papal office : an ecumenical dialogue on
John Paul's encyclical *Ut Unum Sint* (That all may be one) /
edited by Carl E. Braaten and Robert W. Jensen.
p.   cm.
Includes bibliographical references.
ISBN 0-8028-4802-8 (pbk.: alk. paper)
1. Catholic Church. Pope (1978- : John Paul II). *Ut Unum Sint.* 2. Christian
union.   I. Braaten, Carl E., 1929-   II. Jensen, Robert W.
BX1784 .C48   2001

262′.13 — dc21

00-067684

www.eerdmans.com

Contents

CONTENTS

Contributors

Carl E. Braaten, Director, Center for Catholic and Evangelical Theology, Co-editor of *Pro Ecclesia*

Edward Idris Cardinal Cassidy, President, Pontifical Council for Promoting Christian Unity, Vatican City

Brian E. Daley, S.J., Professor, Department of Theology, University of Notre Dame, Notre Dame, Indiana

Joseph Augustine DiNoia, O.P., Secretariat for Doctrine and Pastoral Practices of the United States Bishops' Conference; Professor of Theology, Dominican House of Studies, Washington, D.C. Father DiNoia will become the first director of the newly established Intercultural Forum of the Pope John Paul II Cultural Center, Washington, D. C.

Robert W. Jenson, Senior Scholar for Research, Center of Theological Inquiry, Princeton, New Jersey; Co-editor of *Pro Ecclesia*

Richard J. Mouw, President, Fuller Theological Seminary, Pasadena, California

Stephen W. Sykes, Principal of St. John's College, University of Durham, England.

Geoffrey Wainwright, Cushman Professor of Christian Theology, The Divinity School, Duke University, Durham, North Carolina; Methodist co-chairman of the Joint Council between the Roman Catholic Church and the World Methodist Council

George Weigel, Senior Fellow, Ethics and Public Policy Center, Washington, D.C.

David S. Yeago, Michael C. Peeler Professor of Systematic Theology, Lutheran Theological Southern Seminary, Columbia, South Carolina

Introduction

CARL E. BRAATEN AND ROBERT W. JENSON

This book offers an ecumenically representative response to an important section of Pope John Paul II's 1995 Encyclical Letter, *Ut Unum Sint,* which deals with the "Ministry of Unity of the Bishop of Rome." Here John Paul II exhibits the kind of unremitting commitment to the ecumenical quest for church unity that has characterized his papacy from the beginning. An especially significant aspect of his ministry to full unity has been his pilgrimages to the various churches on different continents. He mentions in particular his visit to the headquarters of the World Council of Churches in Geneva, his ecumenical meetings with the primate of the Anglican Communion at Canterbury Cathedral, with the Ecumenical Patriarch Dimitrios I, and with the Lutheran bishops and archbishops of the Scandinavian and Nordic countries (72). His apostolic visits have included joining in ecumenical celebrations with "churches and ecclesial communities that are not in full communion with the Catholic Church" (n. 42). For him they vividly express the new ecumenical awareness that, despite existing separations, "we all belong to Christ" (42). He speaks of communities that once were rivals and are now "consigning to oblivion the excommunications of the past" (42).

The pope's ecumenical devotion to unity is based on Jesus' high-priestly prayer in Chapter 17 of St. John's Gospel: "This is truly the cornerstone of all prayer: the total and unconditional offering of one's life to the Father, through the Son, in the Holy Spirit. . . . Christ's prayer to the Father is offered as a model for everyone, always and everywhere" (27). John Paul II expresses his confidence that if we would take Christ's call to unity to heart, "that all may be one," "every factor of division can be transcended and overcome in the total gift of self for the sake of the Gospel" (1).

The pope's encyclical letter aims to increase the unity of all Christians until they reach the goal of full communion, and he regards this as the "specific duty of the bishop of Rome as the successor of the apostle Peter" (4). But he does not shrink from acknowledging that "the Catholic Church's conviction that in the ministry of the bishop of Rome she has preserved, in fidelity to the apostolic tradition and the faith of the fathers, the visible sign and guarantor of unity constitutes a difficulty for most other Christians, whose memory is marked by certain painful recollections" (88). Then he adds, "To the extent that we are responsible for these, I join my predecessor Paul VI in asking forgiveness" (88). In this John Paul II echoes the words of Pope Paul VI, who said in 1967: "We are aware that the pope is undoubtedly the greatest obstacle in the path of the *Oecumene.*"

The pope finds encouragement in the fact that the question of papal primacy has become a subject of many of the ecumenical dialogues, most notably in those with Anglicans, Lutherans, and the Orthodox, and that Faith and Order, a movement within the World Council of Churches, has pledged itself to "begin a new study of the question of a universal ministry of Christian unity" (89). Thus John Paul II's invitation to other church leaders and theologians to engage with him in a "patient and fraternal dialogue" on the ministry of the bishop of Rome has a history on which to build.

But what is there to discuss? The pope is not willing to start from scratch. He is convinced that Peter was the first bishop of Rome, that Peter's position of primacy among the Twelve was a direct appointment from Jesus, and that the bishop of Rome is permanently the successor of Peter. Still, he is willing to talk about a "way of exercising the primacy which, while in no way renouncing what is essential to its mission, is nonetheless open to a new situation." (95)

This volume is a kind of thanksgiving offering in appreciation of the pope's effort to promote the unity of all Christians and full communion between churches. The editors are especially pleased that His Eminence, Edward Idris Cardinal Cassidy, President of the Pontifical Council for Promoting Christian Unity, accepted the invitation to deliver the keynote address at the theological conference on "Church Unity and the Papal Office" held at the University of St. Thomas in St. Paul, Minnesota, June 6-8, 1999.

He underscores John Paul II's conviction that ecumenism is an organic part of the life and work of the Catholic Church. Nevertheless, it must always be an ecumenism based on the truths of evangelical faith and catholic doctrine. He signals but does not resolve the paradox that the one to whom the ministry of unity has been entrusted continues to be a source of division and disunity within world Christianity.

Brian Daley, a Jesuit teaching at Notre Dame, offers a tightly woven historical review of the rise of the papal office. That the Petrine ministry came to be centered in Rome derived from the leadership roles of Peter and Paul. Tracing the history of the papacy during the first millennium, Daley's essay offers grist for the kind of creative thinking on primacy for which *Ut Unum Sint* calls.

Stephen Sykes, a bishop of the Anglican Communion, focuses on the issue of power in relation to church leadership, whether episcopcal or papal. The modern church is allergic to the concept of power, looking for euphemistic substitutes. The reality of power is socially unavoidable; it is grounded in a proper theology of creation. It is time for the church to find positive and constructive ways to exercise power.

Geoffrey Wainwright is eminently qualified to speak of *Ut Unum Sint* in light of his work with Faith and Order, where he has played a significant theological role for many years. He offers many ideas to advance the non-polemical style of fraternal dialogue for which the pope's encyclical calls, suggesting that the pope should take the lead in inviting churches to join with him in formulating a new statement of faith to be addressed to the world. Such a process would provide the occasion for the pope to exercise his ministry of unity.

Other contributors enrich the conversation with a variety of approaches. Richard Mouw, president of Fuller Theological Seminary, offers a candid response from an evangelical perspective. The topics of papal primacy and full, visible church unity are not high on the agenda of evangelicals, but they are discovering common ground with Catholics on social issues and missions to the world. David Yeago develops a Lutheran understanding of the papal ministry based on the Lutheran-Catholic dialogues in the United States and those sponsored by the Lutheran World Federation. George Weigel, a Roman Catholic layman and author of a new biography of John Paul II, comments on the struggles in American Catholicism arising from tensions between the hierarchical constitution of the church, dominically authorized, and the American experience, democratically founded. Joseph Augustine DiNoia gave the banquet address on "Ecumenism and the New Evangelization in *Ut Unum Sint*," showing how closely ecumenical work is linked to a passion for evangelization.

> (What follows is that portion of the text of *Ut Unum Sint* that deals with the "Ministry of Unity of the Bishop of Rome." It was reproduced from *Origins, CNS Documentary Service,* June 8, 1995, Vol. 25: No. 4, paragraphs 88-97, pp. 68-70 — The Editors)

Ministry of Unity of the Bishop of Rome

88. Among all the Churches and Ecclesial Communities, the Catholic Church is conscious that she has preserved the ministry of the Successor of the Apostle Peter, the Bishop of Rome, whom God established as her "perpetual and visible principle and foundation of unity"[1] and whom the Spirit sustains in order that he may enable all the others to share in this essential good. In the beautiful expression of Pope St. Gregory the Great, my ministry is that of *servus servorum Dei.* This designation is the best possible safeguard against the risk of separating power (and in particular the primacy) from ministry. Such a separation would contradict the very meaning of power according to the Gospel: "I am among you as one who serves" (Lk. 22:27), says our Lord Jesus Christ, the Head of the Church. On the other hand, as I acknowledged on the important occasion of a visit to the World Council of Churches in Geneva on June 12, 1984, the Catholic Church's conviction that in the ministry of the Bishop of Rome she has preserved, in fidelity to the Apostolic Tradition, and the faith of the Fathers, the visible sign and guarantor of unity, constitutes a difficulty for most other Christians, whose memory is marked by certain painful recollections. To the extent that we are responsible for these, I join my predecessor Paul VI in asking forgiveness.[2]

89. It is nonetheless significant and encouraging that the question of the primacy of the Bishop of Rome has now become a subject of study which is already under way or will be in the near future. It is likewise sig-

---

1. Vatican II, Dogmatic Constitution on the Church *Lumen Gentium,* No. 23.
2. Cf. discourse at the headquarters of the World Council of Churches, Geneva (June 12, 1984), p. 2: *Insegnamenti* VII/1 (1984), p. 1686.

nificant and encouraging that this question appears as an essential theme not only in the theological dialogues in which the Catholic Church is engaging with other Churches and Ecclesial Communities, but also more generally in the ecumenical movement as a whole. Recently the delegates to the Fifth World Assembly of the Commission on Faith and Order of the World Council of Churches, held in Santiago de Campostela, recommended that the commission "begin a new study of the question of a universal ministry of Christian unity."[3] After centuries of bitter controversies, the other Churches and Ecclesial Communities are more and more taking a fresh look at this ministry of unity.[4]

90. The Bishop of Rome is the Bishop of the Church which preserves the mark of the martyrdom of Peter and Paul: "By a mysterious design of Providence it is at Rome that (Peter) concludes his journey in following Jesus, and it is at Rome that he gives his greatest proof of love and fidelity. Likewise Paul, the Apostle of the Gentiles, gives his supreme witness at Rome. In this way the Church of Rome became the church of Peter and Paul."[5]

In the New Testament, the person of Peter has an eminent place. In the first part of the Acts of the Apostles, he appears as the leader and spokesman of the Apostolic College described as "Peter . . . and the Eleven" (2:14; cf. 2:37, 5:29). The place assigned to Peter is based on the words of Christ himself, as they are recorded in the Gospel traditions.

91. The Gospel of Matthew gives a clear outline of the pastoral mission of Peter in the Church: "Blessed are you, Simon Bar-Jonah! For flesh and blood has not revealed this to you, but my Father who is in heaven. And I tell you, you are Peter, and on this rock I will build my Church and the powers of death shall not prevail against it. I will give you the keys of the kingdom of heaven, and whatever you bind on earth shall be bound in heaven, and whatever you loose on earth shall be loosed in heaven" (16:17-

3. World Conference of the Commission on Faith and Order, Report of the Second Section, Santiago de Campostela (1993): *Confessing the One Faith to God's Glory,* 31, 2, Faith and Order paper 166, World Council of Churches, Geneva, 1994, p. 243.

4. To cite only a few examples: Anglican–Roman Catholic International Commission, Final Report, ARCIC-I (September 1981); International Commission for Dialogue between the Disciples of Christ and the Roman Catholic Church, Report (1981); Roman Catholic/Lutheran Joint Commission, The Ministry in the Church (March 13, 1981). The problem takes clear shape in the research conducted by the Joint International Commission for the Theological Dialogue between the Catholic Church and the Orthodox Church.

5. Address to the cardinals and the Roman Curia (June 25, 1985), p. 3.

19). Luke makes clear that Christ urged Peter to strengthen his brethren, while at the same time reminding him of his own human weakness and the need of conversion (cf. 22:31-32). It is just as though, against the backdrop of Peter's human weakness, it were made fully evident that his particular ministry in the Church derives altogether from grace. It is as though the Master especially concerned himself with Peter's conversion as a way of preparing him for the task he was about to give him in his Church, and for this reason was very strict with him. This same role of Peter, similarly linked with a realistic affirmation of his weakness, appears again in the Fourth Gospel: "Simon, son of John, do you love me more than these? . . . Feed my sheep" (Jn. 21:15-19). It is also significant that according to the First Letter of Paul to the Corinthians the risen Christ appears to Cephas and then to the Twelve (cf. 15:5).

It is important to note how the weakness of Peter and Paul clearly shows that the Church is founded upon the infinite power of grace (cf. Mt. 16:17; 2 Cor. 12:7-10). Peter, immediately after receiving his mission, is rebuked with unusual severity by Christ, who tells him: "You are a hindrance to me" (Mt. 16:23). How can we fail to see that the mercy which Peter needs is related to the ministry of that mercy which he is the first to experience? And yet, Peter will deny Jesus three times. The Gospel of John emphasizes that Peter receives the charge of shepherding the flock on the occasion of a threefold profession of love (cf. 21:15-17), which corresponds to his threefold denial (cf. 13:38). Luke, for his part, in the words of Christ already quoted, words which the early tradition will concentrate upon in order to clarify the mission of Peter, insists on the fact that he will have to "strengthen his brethren when he has turned again" (cf. 22:32).

92. As for Paul, he is able to end the description of his ministry with the amazing words which he had heard from the Lord himself: "My grace is sufficient for you, for my power is made perfect in weakness"; consequently, he can exclaim: "When I am weak, then I am strong" (2 Cor. 12:9-10). This is a basic characteristic of the Christian experience.

As the heir to the mission of Peter in the Church, which has been fruitful by the blood of the Princes of the Apostles, the Bishop of Rome exercises a ministry originating in the manifold mercy of God. This mercy converts hearts and pours forth the power of grace where the disciple experiences the bitter taste of his personal weakness and helplessness. The authority proper to this ministry is completely at the service of God's merciful plan, and it must always be seen from this perspective.

6

93. Associating himself with Peter's threefold profession of love, which corresponds to the earlier threefold denial, his Successor knows that he must be a sign of mercy. His is a ministry of mercy, born of an act of Christ's own mercy. The whole lesson of the Gospel must be constantly read anew so that the exercise of the Petrine ministry may lose nothing of its authenticity and transparency.

The Church of God is called by Christ to manifest to a world ensnared by its sins and evil designs that, despite everything, God in his mercy can convert hearts to unity and enable them to enter into communion with him.

94. This service of unity, rooted in the action of divine mercy, is entrusted within the College of Bishops to one among those who have received from the Spirit the task, not of exercising power over the people — as the rulers of the Gentiles and their great men do (cf. Mt. 20:25; Mk. 10:42) — but of leading them toward peaceful pastures. This task can require the offering of one's own life (cf. Jn. 10:11-18). St. Augustine, after showing that Christ is "the one Shepherd, in whose unity all are one," goes on to exhort: "May all shepherds thus be one in the one Shepherd; may they let the one voice of the Shepherd be heard and not a babble of voices ... the voice free of all division, purified of all heresy, that the sheep hear."[6] The mission of the Bishop of Rome within the College of all the Pastors consists precisely in "keeping watch" *(episkopein)*, like a sentinel, so that through the efforts of the Pastors the true voice of Christ the Shepherd may be heard in all the particular Churches. In this way, in each of the particular Churches entrusted to those Pastors, the *una, sancta, catholica et apostolica Ecclesia* is made present. All the Churches are in full and visible communion, because all the Pastors are in communion with Peter and therefore united in Christ.

With the power and the authority without which such an office would be illusory, the Bishop of Rome must ensure the communion of all the Churches. For this reason, he is the first servant of unity. This primacy is exercised on various levels, including vigilance over the handing down of the Word, the celebration of the Liturgy and the Sacraments, the Church's mission, discipline and the Christian life. It is the responsibility of the Successor of Peter to recall the requirements of the common good of the Church, should anyone be tempted to overlook it in the pursuit of per-

6. *Sermon* XLVI, 30: *Corpus Christianorum, Series Latina* 41, p. 557.

sonal interests. He has the duty to admonish, to caution and to declare at times that this or that opinion being circulated is irreconcilable with the unity of faith. When circumstances require it, he speaks in the name of all the Pastors in communion with him. He can also — under very specific conditions clearly laid down by the First Vatican Council — declare *ex cathedra* that a certain doctrine belongs to the deposit of faith.[7] By thus bearing witness to the truth, he serves unity.

95. All this, however, must always be done in communion. When the Catholic Church affirms that the office of the Bishop of Rome corresponds to the will of Christ, she does not separate this office from the mission entrusted to the whole body of Bishops, who are also "vicars and ambassadors of Christ."[8] The Bishop of Rome is a member of the "college," and the Bishops are his brothers in the ministry.

Whatever relates to the unity of all Christian communities clearly forms part of the concerns of the primacy. As Bishop of Rome I am fully aware, as I have reaffirmed in the present Encyclical Letter, that Christ ardently desires the full and visible communion of all those Communities in which, by virtue of God's faithfulness, his Spirit dwells. I am convinced that I have a particular responsibility in this regard, above all in acknowledging the ecumenical aspirations of the majority of the Christian Communities and in heeding the request made of me to find a way of exercising the primacy which, while in no way renouncing what is essential to its mission, is nonetheless open to a new situation. For a whole millennium Christians were united in a "brotherly fraternal communion of faith and sacramental life. . . . If disagreements in belief and discipline arose among them, the Roman See acted by common consent as moderator."[9]

In this way the primacy exercised its office of unity. When addressing the Ecumenical Patriarch His Holiness Dimitrios I, I acknowledged my awareness that "for a great variety of reasons, and against the will of all concerned, what should have been a service sometimes manifested itself in a very different light. But . . . it is out of a desire to obey the will of Christ truly that I recognize that as Bishop of Rome I am called to exercise that ministry. . . . I insistently pray the Holy Spirit to shine his light upon us,

7. Cf. Vatican Ecumenical Council I, Dogmatic Constitution on the Church of Christ *Pastor Aeternus: Enchiridion Symbolorum,* Denz.-Schon., 3074.

8. *Lumen Gentium,* No. 27.

9. *Unitatis Redintegratio,* No. 14.

enlightening all the Pastors and theologians of our Churches, that we may seek — together, of course — the forms in which this ministry may accomplish a service of love recognized by all concerned."[10]

96. This is an immense task, which we cannot refuse and which I cannot carry out by myself. Could not the real but imperfect communion existing between us persuade Church leaders and their theologians to engage with me in a patient and fraternal dialogue on this subject, a dialogue in which, leaving useless controversies behind, we could listen to one another, keeping before us only the will of Christ for his Church and allowing ourselves to be deeply moved by his plea "that they may all be one . . . so that the world may believe that you have sent me" (Jn. 17:21)?

97. The Catholic Church, both in her praxis and in her solemn documents, holds that the communion of the particular Churches with the Church of Rome, and of their Bishops with the Bishop of Rome, is — in God's plan — an essential requisite of full and visible communion. Indeed full communion, of which the Eucharist is the highest sacramental manifestation, needs to be visibly expressed in a ministry in which all the Bishops recognize that they are united in Christ and all the faithful find confirmation for their faith. The first part of the Acts of the Apostles presents Peter as the one who speaks in the name of the apostolic group and who serves the unity of the community — all the while respecting the authority of James, the head of the Church in Jerusalem. The function of Peter must continue in the Church so that under her sole Head, who is Jesus Christ, she may be visibly present in the world as the communion of all his disciples.

Do not many of those involved in ecumenism today feel a need for such a ministry? A ministry which presides in truth and love so that the ship — that beautiful symbol which the World Council of Churches has chosen as its emblem — will not be buffeted by the storms and will one day reach its haven.

---

10. Homily in the Vatican basilica in the presence of Dimitrios I, archbishop of Constantinople and ecumenical patriarch (Dec. 6, 1987), 3:AAS 8 (1988), p. 714.

Ut Unum Sint in Ecumenical Perspective

EDWARD IDRIS CARDINAL CASSIDY

Pope John Paul II published his encyclical letter *Ut Unum Sint*[1] just four years ago on May 25, 1995, the Solemnity of the Ascension of the Lord. It has made a vital contribution to the ecumenical movement as the first encyclical letter ever written on the subject of ecumenism. It is also one of the very few documents issued officially by the churches on their commitment to and vision of this movement, which the Second Vatican Council has described as "fostered by the grace of the Holy Spirit, for the restoration of unity among all Christians."[2]

In fact, this encyclical, along with the *Directory for the Application of Principles and Norms on Ecumenism,* present to the ecumenical movement an extensive vision of how one church understands the ecumenical movement: its goal, the means to achieve that goal, its successes so far, and the work still to be done. These are undoubtedly key texts of the twentieth-century ecumenical movement, for while they are addressed primarily to the members of the Catholic Church, they offer a challenge to other churches at a time when there are many factors distracting Christians from the quest for visible unity, and when questions are being asked about the health of the ecumenical movement. Certainly no other papal encyclical has been so widely distributed and studied outside the Catholic Church as has *Ut Unum Sint.* This ecumenical dialogue, jointly sponsored by the

---

1. Pope John Paul II, Encyclical Letter *Ut Unum Sint* on Commitment to Ecumenism. Vatican City: Libreria Editrice Vaticana, 1995.

2. Decree of the Second Vatican Council *Unitatis Redintegratio,* No. 1.

Center for Catholic and Evangelical Theology and the Archdiocese of St. Paul and Minneapolis, is itself proof of the importance of the contribution that the papal document *Ut Unum Sint* has made to the ecumenical movement over the past four years. In this keynote address I would like to reflect briefly on the essential elements of this contribution, and then seek to give an idea of the comments and reactions that the Pontifical Council has received.

The very title of the encyclical informs the reader that its primary scope is to insist on the commitment of the Catholic Church to the search for Christian unity. The Second Vatican Council, in the Decree on Ecumenism *Unitatis Redintegratio,* urged "all the Catholic faithful to recognize the signs of the times and to take an active and intelligent part in the work of ecumenism."[3] The Council Fathers saw this as the logical consequence of what they described as "multiple efforts being made in many parts of the world, under the inspiring grace of the Holy Spirit, through prayer, word and action to attain that fullness of unity which Jesus Christ desires."[4] Pope John Paul II understands this Council decision as irreversible, and in his encyclical describes the ecumenical way as the way of the church. He sees the unity that we seek as being something "which the Lord has bestowed on his Church and in which he seeks to embrace all people," and which therefore "stands at the very heart of Christ's mission" and "belongs to the very essence of the community of his disciples."[5] "Thus," he writes, "it is absolutely clear that ecumenism [. . .] *is not just some sort of 'appendix,'* which is added to the Church's traditional activity. Rather, ecumenism is an organic part of her life and work, and consequently must pervade all that she is and does; it must be like the fruit borne by a healthy and flourishing tree which grows to its full stature."[6]

These and other similar statements in the encyclical[7] go beyond the Catholic Church to reach out and call on all Christians to reflect. It seems vital for the future of the search for Christian unity that Christians see this

---

3. *Unitatis Redintegratio,* No. 4.
4. *Unitatis Redintegratio,* No. 4.
5. *Ut Unum Sint,* No. 9.
6. *Ut Unum Sint,* No. 20.
7. *Ut Unum Sint,* No. 9: "to believe in Christ means to desire unity; to desire unity means to desire the Church; to desire the Church means to desire the communion of grace which corresponds to the Father's plan from all eternity. Such is the meaning of Christ's prayer: '*Ut Unum Sint.*'"

quest as indeed "an organic part of the life and work" of their communities, and not just as something merely added on to their Church's traditional activity. Much work has to be done in all our communities before we can confidently state that the aspiration to unity is thus solidly based.

Ecumenism is not to be seen then as a program of the Catholic Church; ecumenism is in the nature of being the Catholic Church. The Church cannot be true to itself unless it is ecumenical.[8] This is a truth too little appreciated by many Catholics. The encyclical points out that the same "transparency and prudence of faith" that require us to avoid compromise on questions of faith urge us "to reject a half-hearted commitment to unity and, even more, a prejudicial opposition or a defeatism which tends to see everything in negative terms."[9]

Another important feature of the encyclical is the confirmation that this commitment is to the full, visible unity of the Christian family. This comes at a time when, within the ecumenical movement, doubts have been expressed about the possibility of such a goal ever being reached. More and more we notice a tendency to concentrate on a more pragmatic approach that would limit the aims of those engaged in ecumenical searching to intermediate or short-term goals, leaving aside, if not renouncing, any attempt to aim at the ultimate goal of full, visible unity. In stating that *"Christ calls his disciples to unity,"*[10] His Holiness makes it clear that:

> The greater mutual understanding and the doctrinal convergences already achieved between us, which have resulted in an affective and effective growth of communion, cannot suffice for the conscience of Christians who profess that the Church is one, holy, catholic and apostolic. The ultimate goal of the ecumenical movement is to re-establish full visible unity among all the baptized.[11]

That does not mean, of course, that we should neglect or undervalue intermediate or short-term goals. It is obvious that for the pope, the search for unity is a process, a joint ascent to the summit of a high and challenging mountain, which offers at each step forward a new and exciting vision. Rev. John Hotchkin sees us now at a stage in this journey which he de-

8. Cf. Richard John Neuhaus, *Crisis* (September 1995), pp. 25-27.
9. *Ut Unum Sint,* No. 79.
10. *Ut Unum Sint,* No. 1.
11. *Ut Unum Sint,* No. 77.

scribes as "phased reconciliation."[12] What concerns the Catholic Church is the growing tendency to leave aside the idea of *visible* unity and to replace it with vague notions such as "conciliar fellowship."

The reason for the movement away from the pursuit of full, visible unity within the ecumenical movement, which has in the past always been the goal of the Faith and Order Commission of the World Council of churches, is to be found, I believe, mainly in frustration and disillusionment at the slow rate of progress in this search for greater communion. The difficulties that the churches are encountering in this quest bring a natural tendency to limit the goal. *Ut Unum Sint* is a response to this challenge.

Right at the beginning of the encyclical, Pope John Paul II seeks to encourage those who may be victims of frustration or disillusionment by thanking the Lord "that he has led us to make progress along the path of unity and communion between Christians, a path so difficult but full of joy."[13] To illustrate this important point, the encyclical devotes all of Chapter Two to the "fruits of dialogue," noting that Christians of one confession no longer consider other Christians as enemies or strangers. Already the Second Vatican Council had solemnly declared:

> All those justified by faith through baptism are incorporated into Christ. They therefore have a right to be honored by the title of Christian, and are properly regarded as brothers in the Lord by the sons and daughters of the Catholic Church.[14]

The pope points out that new expressions are now used to indicate new attitudes based on a common awareness "that we all belong to Christ. . . . The 'universal brotherhood' of Christians has become a firm ecumenical conviction."[15] His Holiness speaks of brotherhood rediscovered, a brotherhood that "is not the consequence of a large-hearted philanthropy or a vague family spirit [but] is rooted in recognition of the oneness of baptism and the subsequent duty to glorify God in his work."[16] These new

---

12. John Hotchkin, "The Ecumenical Movement's Third Stage," *Origins* 8 (June 1995), p. 336.

13. *Ut Unum Sint*, No. 2.

14. *Unitatis Redintegratio*, No. 3.

15. *Ut Unum Sint*, No. 42.

16. *Ut Unum Sint*, No. 42.

attitudes, moreover, lead not only to new words but also to new works in various forms of cooperation and solidarity in the service of humanity.

Renewed and frequent contacts between the churches have strengthened the bonds that unite them and have led to substantial progress in the various theological dialogues. "The process has been slow and arduous, yet a source of great joy."[17] The real though imperfect communion that the Second Vatican Council found to be existing between the baptized has continued to grow and be strengthened, especially through prayer and dialogue. Those involved in the ecumenical ministry have seen important fruits in their own lives from being so involved, including Pope John Paul II himself.

His Holiness concludes his reflection on the progress made in the theological dialogue with the following evaluation:

> This dialogue has been and continues to be fruitful and full of promise. The topics suggested by the Council Decree have already been addressed, or will be in the future. The reflections of the various bilateral dialogues, conducted with a dedication that deserves the praise of all those committed to ecumenism, have concentrated on many disputed questions surrounding such topics as Baptism, the Eucharist, the ordained ministry, the sacramentality and authority of the Church, and apostolic succession. As a result, unexpected possibilities for resolving these questions have come to light, while at the same time there has been a realization that certain questions need to be studied more deeply.[18]

How much further do we have to go? This is the title of Chapter Three of the pope's encyclical. In No. 79 of this third chapter of his encyclical, His Holiness identifies the areas in need of fuller study before a true consensus of faith can be achieved:

(1) The relationship between Sacred Scripture, as the highest authority in matters of faith, and Sacred Tradition, as indispensable to the interpretation of the Word of God
(2) The Eucharist, as the Sacrament of the Body and Blood of Christ, an offering of praise to the Father, the sacrificial memorial and Real Presence of Christ and the sanctifying outpouring of the Holy Spirit

17. *Ut Unum Sint,* No. 51.
18. *Ut Unum Sint,* No. 69.

(3) Ordination, as a Sacrament, to the threefold ministry of the episcopate, presbyterate and diaconate

(4) The Magisterium of the Church, entrusted to the Pope and the Bishops in communion with him, understood as a responsibility and an authority exercised in the name of Christ for teaching and safeguarding the faith

(5) The Virgin Mary, as Mother of God and Icon of the Church, the spiritual Mother who intercedes for Christ's disciples and for all humanity.

In this connection, a most interesting aspect of the encyclical is the section entitled "Contribution of the Catholic Church to the Quest for Christian Unity" (No. 86 and No. 87), which is immediately followed by a reflection of the Holy Father on the ministry of unity of the bishop of Rome (No. 88 to No. 96). This is the heart of our present dialogue on church unity and the papal office.

This aspect of the search for unity presents Pope John Paul II with a dramatic paradox. While expressing his strong commitment to ecumenism, both as an individual believer and as head of the Catholic Church, he realizes that in the view of many of those he wishes to challenge with this encyclical, the primacy that he exercises as the successor of Peter is one of the principal obstacles to that unity. The ministry of the bishop of Rome is primarily a ministry of unity, yet one that can be a source of "painful recollections" for most other Christians. His Holiness joins his predecessor Pope Paul VI in asking forgiveness "to the extent that we are responsible for these."[19]

At the same time, the pope is encouraged by the fact that, after centuries of bitter controversies, other churches and ecclesial communities are taking a fresh look at the question of the primacy of the bishop of Rome. At the conclusion of a profound reflection on the role of the papacy in the search for unity, Pope John Paul II states:

> I am convinced that I have a particular responsibility in this regard, above all in acknowledging the ecumenical aspirations of the majority of the Christian Communities and in heeding the request made of me to find a way of exercising the primacy which, while in no way re-

19. *Ut Unum Sint,* No. 88.

15

nouncing what is essential to its mission, is nonetheless open to a new situation.[20]

In his homily during the Mass celebrated in St. Peter's Basilica, in the presence of His Holiness, Patriarch Dimitrios I of Constantinople, on December 6, 1987, Pope John Paul II had already expressed his hope that "the Holy Spirit may shine his light upon us, enlightening all the Pastors and theologians of our churches, that we may seek — together of course — the forms in which this ministry may accomplish a service of love recognized by all concerned."[21] While acknowledging now that this is "an immense task, which we cannot refuse and which I cannot carry out on by myself," Pope John Paul II renews his appeal to church leaders and their theologians to engage with him in a patient and fraternal dialogue on this subject, "a dialogue in which, leaving useless controversies behind, we could listen to one another, keeping before us only the will of Christ for his Church, and allowing ourselves to be deeply moved by his plea 'that they may all be one . . . so that the world may believe that you have sent me' (Jn 17:21)."[22]

These reflections have elicited great interest and many comments. Rev. Richard John Neuhaus has written:

> I am confident that we would not go wrong in understanding the Holy Father to be saying that unity is more important than jurisdiction. Christians in the East have been waiting a thousand years to hear a Bishop of Rome say that, and now it is being said.[23]

An official press release of the World Council of Churches, published immediately after the appearance of the encyclical, "warmly welcomed the encyclical," noting in particular "the strong commitment to ecumenism by the Pope and, through him, the Roman Catholic Church." It expresses satisfaction that the encyclical "affirms a number of WCC initiatives" and "contains a strong theology of baptism which provides for the fellowship (koinonia) we already share."[24] On the question of primacy, the secretary-

---

20. *Ut Unum Sint*, No. 95.

21. *Ut Unum Sint*, No. 95. Quote is from the homily in the Vatican Basilica in the presence of Dimitrios I, December 6, 1987; *AAS* 80 (1988): 714.

22. *Ut Unum Sint*, No. 96.

23. Richard John Neuhaus, *Crisis* (September 1995), p. 25.

24. World Council of Churches Office of Communication, press release, June 1, 1995. Georges Lemopoulos, Executive Secretary of the WCC for Church and Ecumenical Rela-

general of the WCC, Dr. Konrad Raiser, has written that, while the encyclical raises the question of "how to find a way of exercising primacy which is open to the new ecumenical situation, without rejecting anything essential from its mission," he can see "no sign yet that the pope is ready to consider the necessary self-relativization of his primacy." For Raiser, the papal office remains the "foremost obstacle" to reunification.[25]

On January 29, 1998, the Faith and Order Commission of the World Council of churches, after much reflection and debate, sent the Pontifical Council for Promoting Christian Unity an official response to *Ut Unum Sint*. The commission expresses gratitude for the papal document and sees a certain harmony there with the work of Faith and Order, which is specifically recognized in the encyclical. The Faith and Order response notes with satisfaction the commitment to ecumenism and the "sense of movement" toward full visible unity that characterize the document, together with the stress on "the need for interior conversion" and for "continual reformation" in Nos. 15 and 16. The commission acknowledges particularly "the spirit of humility which runs through the encyclical" and its emphasis on seeking necessary and sufficient visible unity (No. 78) as a clear endorsement of legitimate diversity.

While appreciating "the combination of personal courtesy and theological candor with which the encyclical speaks of other churches and Ecclesial Communions," the Faith and Order response considers unsatisfactory some of the references made to these churches in the encyclical. It notes, however, that this is balanced to some extent by "the statement that the martyrs who died for their Christian faith, no matter what Christian tradition they belong to, as well as the saints of all our traditions, are already in perfect communion (No. 84)." The response further speaks of much similarity between the issues that it is grappling with and those indicated in *Ut Unum Sint*. One of these is of course primacy, and satisfaction is expressed that this ministry of unity is referred to as one of service and not one of power.

Responses from the Orthodox churches have been rather few and, given the importance of the primacy for the Roman Catholic–Orthodox

---

tions, added a longer comment, confirming this positive reaction and referring to two other documents of Pope John Paul II, *Tertio Millennio Adveniente* and *Orientale Lumen*, that also illustrate Pope John Paul's "ecumenical commitment."

25. Interview with the Polish Catholic weekly *Tygodnik Powszechny*, reported by Catholic News Service, July 9, 1996.

theological dialogue, rather disappointing. In a limited comment, Ecumenical Patriarch Bartholomew I of Constantinople has stated that the encyclical *Ut Unum Sint* would "undoubtedly have been accepted with gratitude" by all denominations if the Catholic Church had been ready to consider the papal office in line with the "pentarchy." "This means," he said, "if the Church and its theologians had been prepared to see the pope as coordinator and senior leader without extremes and theologically mistaken demands for a world primacy in the jurisdictional sense — or even worse, for personal infallibility over the whole Church and independently of it."[26]

I would just mention two other important responses from the Orthodox Church that merit special attention. Immediately after the publication of the encyclical, Metropolitan Damaskinos of Switzerland contributed a long and very positive article to the French newspaper *La Croix* and issued a shorter version of the same to all the mass media. He did not hesitate to state that this encyclical letter was a remarkable and constructive contribution by His Holiness Pope John Paul II "to the search which the Catholic Church is carrying out with other churches and ecclesial communities for the re-establishment of the unity of all the baptized."[27] Olivier Clément, a professor at the Orthodox Institut Sainte-Serge, Paris, finds that the encyclical gives the ecumenical movement a properly spiritual foundation, "a method based on common prayer in the sincere discovery of the other, and on repentance." It should signify, he hopes, "the end of accusation of the other."[28]

For its part, the Church of England officially welcomed the encyclical immediately after its publication with the following statement issued by Lambeth Palace: "At a time when there is growing impatience with the ecumenical movement and a tendency to give up on the search for visible unity, this urgent call by the Pope to continue along a path which is difficult yet full of joy encourages us to continue with greater determination." The statement found much in the encyclical with which Anglicans could agree "wholeheartedly," and expressed readiness "to exploring more deeply the ministry of unity which belongs to the Bishop of Rome, in the light of

26. Interview with the Polish Catholic weekly *Tygodnik Powszechny*, reported by Catholic News Service, July 9, 1996.

27. *La Croix*, June 1, 1995.

28. *Le Monde*, June 1, 1995.

the work currently being undertaken by the second Anglican–Roman Catholic International Commission (ARCIC II)."[29] In addition, several later Anglican responses to the encyclical pointed out the many positive elements that they found in the encyclical, noting in particular the emphasis on spiritual ecumenism and the references in the papal document to legitimate diversity within the unity that we seek.[30]

One of the most important responses to *Ut Unum Sint* came from the House of Bishops of the Church of England in June 1997.[31] This document would merit a conference by itself. The House of Bishops sees the encyclical itself as "a source of great joy" and as an indication of "the Pope's desire to make his ministry a service of unity to the whole Church." The response welcomes the Pope's commitment to ecumenism and his "clear assertion that visible unity is God's will for the Church," together with the "insistence throughout the encyclical on the inseparable relation between the mission and unity of the Church." The bishops refer at some length to the work of ARCIC I and ARCIC II, and offer valuable reflections on the teaching office of the Church and decision making when churches are separated. A section entitled "Real but Imperfect Communion," discusses the expression *subsistit in* of *Lumen Gentium* and *Unitatis Redintegratio* at some length. The document looks forward to further exploration on this expression and on "the witness of the martyrs and their perfect communion in Christ even if the churches from which they come have not been fully united."

Special attention has been given by the House of Bishops of the Church of England to what they see as central to dialogue between Roman Catholics and other Christians, namely the role of the bishop of Rome in the church. They state that "Anglicans and Catholics are at one in their understanding of the episcopate as a ministry involving not only oversight of each local church but also a care for the universal communion of which each church is a member." Recalling ARCIC I's statement on the office of universal primacy, the bishops affirm:

---

29. Press release, Communications Unit of the General Synod of the Church of England, London, No. PR 17/95.

30. Canon Roger Greenacre, Chancellor of Chichester Cathedral, in *La Croix,* June 1, 1995; Rev. Robert Macfarlane of Chicago in *Ecumenical Trends,* January 1996; Rev. Douglas Brown, Director of the Anglican Centre, Rome, *Radiogiornale Vaticano,* June 7, 1995.

31. *May They All Be One: A Response of the House of Bishops of the Church of England to Ut Unum Sint.* House of Bishops Occasional Paper GS Misc. 495.

Anglicans are thus by no means opposed to the principle and practice of a personal ministry at the world level in the service of unity. Indeed, increasingly their experience of the Anglican Communion is leading them to appreciate the proper need, alongside communal and collegial ministries, for a personal service of unity in the faith.

The House of Bishops would not rule out "the universal primacy of the bishop of Rome as the person who particularly signifies the unity and the universality of the Church" and they would be ready "to acknowledge his special responsibilities for maintaining unity in the truth and ordering things in love," but they would have reservations in so doing. They note the serious obstacles that still exist "because of the present Roman Catholic understanding of the jurisdiction attributed to the primacy of the Bishop of Rome" over the whole church. They make it clear, however, that "this is not an argument for a primacy of honour only, or for the exclusion from a universal primacy of the authority necessary for a world-wide ministry in the service of unity."

The Lutheran World Federation also gave the encyclical a warm welcome. Gottfried Brakemeir, who was president of the LWF at the time, stated that the encyclical "deserves to be received with gratitude" and expressed the hope that it may "contribute to accelerating the approximation of the churches towards the visible unity of the body of Christ."[32] In a special press release, the secretary-general of the Lutheran World Federation, Rev. Ismael Noko, affirms that "Lutherans can only be grateful for this positive and forceful restatement of the commitment of the Roman Catholic Church to Christian unity. . . . The Roman Catholic Church is unmatched in its public commitment to the visible unity of the Christ's church." Noko applauds the pope's proposal of dialogue to review the future role of the papacy. He does not lament the special attention given in the encyclical to the Catholic-Orthodox dialogue, but sees as "especially welcome for Lutherans . . . an unprecedented emphasis on the work of Faith and Order, the bilateral dialogues with churches separated from Rome in the Reformation of the 16th century and the ecclesial understanding of ecumenical co-operation in meeting human need."[33]

On a visit to Pope John Paul II, Archbishop Hammar of Uppsala, presented the pope with an official response to *Ut Unum Sint* from the

32. Lutheran World Information, No. 11/95.
33. Press release, Lutheran World Federation, May 31, 1995.

Bishops' Conference of the Church of Sweden. The response recalls the visit of Pope John Paul II to Sweden just ten years ago, a visit that is mentioned no less than three times in the encyclical (Nos. 24, 25, 72). The bishops of Sweden welcome *Ut Unum Sint* "with its strong emphasis on the ecumenical task, given by Christ, as God's will and as God's gift to his church."[34] There is much in the encyclical with which they can agree, including "the analysis of the hindrances and stumbling-blocks . . . on the road to ecumenism" and "a number of positive aspects concerning results reached on the way towards greater visible unity, not least through the inter-confessional theological dialogues."[35]

The Swedish bishops have two particular difficulties with the encyclical. First, they sense "a hierarchy of churches" reflected in the attitude of the Roman Catholic Church toward other churches and denominations. Following on the statement made by the Second Vatican Council in the decree *Unitatis Redintegratio,* the encyclical *Ut Unum Sint* asserts once again that "the one Church of Christ subsists in the Catholic Church." This creates in principle two problems for the Church of Sweden: it is difficult for dialogue to take place on an equal footing when one of the partners is already from the start regarded as inferior or defective. "Ultimately, that militates against the spirit of human dignity, fairness and truth, which the Pope himself invokes in the description of the prerequisites of the dialogue . . . where each party recognizes the other as a *partner*."[36] The second difficulty is closely connected to the first, and concerns the use by the pope of the term "Catholic" as referring to the Roman Catholic Church.

The Swedish bishops note with satisfaction the important role given in the encyclical to the sacrament of baptism. Still, they insist that the mutual recognition of baptism by the churches should open the way to some degree of recognition of each other's churches and ministries, and of their Eucharist. They consider the issues of ordination and ministry as still being "the greatest difficulty on the ecumenical road."[37]

---

34. "A Response to the Encyclical Letter *Ut Unum Sint* from the Bishops' Conference, Church of Sweden," p. 3.

35. "A Response to the Encyclical Letter *Ut Unum Sint* from the Bishops' Conference, Church of Sweden," p. 4.

36. "A Response to the Encyclical Letter *Ut Unum Sint* from the Bishops' Conference, Church of Sweden," p. 5.

37. "A Response to the Encyclical Letter *Ut Unum Sint* from the Bishops' Conference, Church of Sweden," p. 7.

A large part of the Swedish document is dedicated to "the Ministry of Peter."[38] The invitation to a dialogue on this question is seen as "an historic new initiative by Pope John Paul II . . . on what is a key issue for us all." The bishops refer to Luther's various attitudes toward the papacy and to developments regarding primacy in the Roman Catholic–Lutheran dialogue. Like the bishops of the Church of England, they express an openness towards a special ministry for Peter in the church, "while remembering that the historical connection between St. Peter and the Bishop of Rome has not always been recognized by the Reformed churches,"[39] and acknowledging that from the time of Luther, "the Lutheran tradition, of which the Church of Sweden is a part, has treated the issue of the ministry and position of the Pope negatively and with great scepticism."[40] At the same time, the Swedish document acknowledges the developments in Lutheran–Roman Catholic dialogue in this regard and declares:

> Through the publication of *Ut Unum Sint* the situation has changed again. New steps ought to be possible, in fact, by drawing closer to Luther's wishes — if, as a Lutheran, one wants to read the text in such a way that the Word of God and the gospel is at the center. Concerning the doctrine of justification, the Roman Catholic Church and the Lutheran World Federation have reached almost total agreement. This provides us with a new and more promising situation for continued talks, including on the issues of ecclesiology and on the ordained ministry, and most particularly with regard to the ministry of the successor of Peter.[41]

The bishops of Sweden raise a number of questions concerning the ecclesiological significance and nature of the primacy of Peter and conclude by suggesting that "in order to make progress, the concept of *collegiality* must probably be further developed."[42] They suggest that an ideal bal-

---

38. "A Response to the Encyclical Letter *Ut Unum Sint* from the Bishops' Conference, Church of Sweden," pp. 8-12.

39. "A Response to the Encyclical Letter *Ut Unum Sint* from the Bishops' Conference, Church of Sweden," p. 8.

40. "A Response to the Encyclical Letter *Ut Unum Sint* from the Bishops' Conference, Church of Sweden," p. 8.

41. "A Response to the Encyclical Letter *Ut Unum Sint* from the Bishops' Conference, Church of Sweden," p. 9.

42. "A Response to the Encyclical Letter *Ut Unum Sint* from the Bishops' Conference, Church of Sweden," p. 11.

ance between "papalism" and "conciliarism" could be found were the bishops to exercise the teaching authority of the church together with the pope, as bishop of Rome, at their head. For them, "it is only in this light that the ministry of the successor of Peter is ecumenically possible, as an expression of the College of Bishops and incorporated in the People of God."[43] They add,

> This is our vision in a hopeful ecumenical perspective. It leads towards the model of a conciliar communion, with churches in close consultation and wide sacramental communion, where the apostolicity and catholicity of the Church is made obvious; made visible in a variety of ways, including in the doctrine of the ministry, and which in a dynamic manner creates space for ecumenical pluralism, having an *episkopē* function, which at its head also makes a symbolic petrine function possible, ecumenically understood and realized according to the possible interpretations of both the Bible and the universal ecclesiastical traditions. The multiplicity of churches present is the greatest challenge for the Roman Catholic Church, with its tendencies to regimentation, just as unity will probably be the greatest challenge for many of the other churches, including the Church of Sweden, divided as they are.[44]

In the concluding paragraphs the bishops of Sweden join Pope John Paul II in stating that "ecumenism is an unavoidable task as an expression of the love of God in Christ,"[45] and they affirm,

> In spite of unavoidable difficulties on the way ahead, we therefore wish to continue to pray for grace and confidence to journey ahead together with the pope and the Roman Catholic Church towards the fullness of unity.[46]

Reactions from other Reformed and Evangelical communions have been far less enthusiastic, especially with regard to the question of pri-

---

43. "A Response to the Encyclical Letter *Ut Unum Sint* from the Bishops' Conference, Church of Sweden," p. 11.

44. "A Response to the Encyclical Letter *Ut Unum Sint* from the Bishops' Conference, Church of Sweden," p. 12.

45. "A Response to the Encyclical Letter *Ut Unum Sint* from the Bishops' Conference, Church of Sweden," p. 13.

46. "A Response to the Encyclical Letter *Ut Unum Sint* from the Bishops' Conference, Church of Sweden," p. 13.

macy. This is readily understandable. It is indeed difficult to find a place for the primacy of the bishop of Rome in an ecclesiology that does not normally have a significant role for the ministry of the ordained bishop. Milan Opocensky, general secretary of the World Alliance of Reformed Churches (WARC), in an early comment on the encyclical, gave a broad welcome to the initiative to strengthen and deepen ecumenical cooperation but found it "unthinkable to accept the papacy as a symbol of unity among Christians."[47] Lukas Vischer, a Swiss Reformed theologian and former director of Faith and Order at the World Council of Churches, said that the encyclical presented a "dilemma" for churches of the Reformation. In an article in the French newspaper *Le Monde*, Vischer wrote,

> On the one hand we can only welcome the fundamental convictions contained in the text. To a large extent they correspond with the convictions declared by the World Council over the years. On the other hand, the text comes from the supreme authority of the Roman Catholic Church where, according to Catholic doctrine, the ministry of the pope is crucial to the re-establishment of unity, and thus the encyclical necessarily becomes a plea for the ministry of unity of the pope.[48]

Vischer doubted that this vision of the pope's ministry of unity could be put at the service of the church, and expressed his conviction that the Reformation churches cannot in good conscience associate themselves with such a vision. A very recent symposium of the Evangelical Faculty of Vienna found no place in reformed thinking for a personal primacy, or for dogmas in the church.

Not all Reformed comment has been so negative. Rev. Paul Crow, the Ecumenical Officer of the Christian Church (Disciples of Christ), has stated:

> I'm one of those who believe the office of the papacy is not only essential for the Roman Catholic Church, but is an important office for all Christians. We can debate him (Pope John Paul II) . . . but it's not an office Protestants can ignore. His invitation to rethink how he exercises that role is thus an invitation to shared ministry.[49]

47. Press release ENI-95-0122, Ecumenical News International.
48. *Le Monde,* June 1, 1995.
49. *Boston Globe,* May 31, 1995.

Before concluding, I would like to mention two Roman Catholic reflections that might help us in our deliberations. A roundtable discussion at the Theological Institute Don Orione on Monte Mario in Rome produced the conviction that, if the pope's appeal to theologians and leaders of other Christian churches and ecclesial communions is to find a positive response, then the Petrine ministry must succeed in achieving a greater harmony than is evident at present between the concept of primacy and other gospel values, such as the Word and the Spirit, the missionary commitment, collegiality, subsidiarity and community participation, and the spiritual and mystical perspective of papal authority.[50] Another important Roman Catholic contribution on the subject came on the visit of Cardinal Carlo Maria Martini, Archbishop of Milan, to His All-Holiness Patriarch of Constantinople Bartholomaios I, on May 8, 1998. While these remarks of the Cardinal refer to more general Orthodox-Catholic relations, they can, I believe, be applied specifically to the question of the primacy of the bishop of Rome.

> The need of purifying the memory and healing still-open wounds of the past should not be separated from the need to discern, in a side-by-side comparison of our two traditions, which of our differences are the result of the work of the one who divides or of the sin of man, and which, on the other hand, come from the Spirit who diversifies forms so as to bring them together in a unity that is no longer carnal but spiritual.[51]

I would like to conclude by stating my conviction that the encyclical *Ut Unum Sint* has made a most valuable contribution to the ecumenical movement as the Jubilee year 2000 approaches. It has made clear that as disciples of Christ, we are called to unity, and this not for some personal motive or satisfaction of our own, but "so that the world may believe" (John 17:21). "How indeed," asks Pope John Paul II, "can we proclaim the Gospel of reconciliation without at the same time being committed to working for reconciliation between Christians? . . . When non-believers meet missionaries who do not agree among themselves, even though they all appeal to Christ, will they be in a position to receive the true message? Will they not think that the Gospel is the cause of division, despite the fact that it is presented as the fundamental law of love?"[52]

50. *Radiovaticana Radiogiornale* 42, no. 147 (May 27, 1998), p. 9.
51. Translation from an unpublished copy of the Cardinal's message.
52. *Ut Unum Sint*, No. 98.

The way ahead will not be easy. The path to unity and communion among Christians is indeed — as the pope knows all too well — "difficult but so full of joy."[53] Yet the encyclical closes on a note full of faith and hope:

> There is no doubt that the Holy Spirit is active in this endeavor and is leading the Church to the full realization of the Father's plan, in conformity with the will of Christ. This will was expressed with heartfelt urgency in the prayer which, according to the Fourth Gospel, he uttered at the moment when he entered upon the saving mystery of the Passover. Just as he did then, today too Christ calls everyone to renew their commitment to work for full and visible communion.[54]

It is the response of Christians to this call on which the future of the ecumenical movement will depend in the long run. Nothing is lacking from the Lord. He has given us his Spirit to guide and inspire us. The big question remains: to what degree are we ready to listen to what the Spirit is saying to the churches today?

53. *Ut Unum Sint,* No. 2.
54. *Ut Unum Sint,* No. 100.

The Ministry of Primacy and the Communion of Churches

BRIAN E. DALEY, S.J.

Diversity is one of the great preoccupations of our age. In businesses, schools, churches, and even advertising, American culture has witnessed, since at least the mid-1960s, a steadily increasing emphasis on the principle that the accidental differences between individuals in our society — differences of race and gender, certainly, but also of religious and moral conviction, talent, intelligence, taste, and habitual behavior — ought not to be seen as grounds for treating those individuals differently, or to suggest differences in their intrinsic social and human worth. It has become a familiar refrain in academic discourse for universities to assert that the construction of a racially, ethnically, and socially diverse student body is an indispensable element of a healthy environment for modern education, even if it involves discriminatory enrollment practices. We now tend to idealize the harmonious modern society in terms of the iconic posters of the United Colors of Benetton: a row of smiling, energetic young people, curiously homogeneous in dress, ambitions, affluence, and implied social class, but deliberately varied and proportionately balanced in color, gender and national background.

The main reason for our public pursuit of diversity, in America at least, is obviously the inequality in opportunity and legal protection that for so long ruled in our society. American egalitarianism in the past, so celebrated by Tocqueville and other early observers, was largely an egalitarianism among middle-class white Protestant males. But there is also, I

27

think, a deeper, less obvious aspect to this new social ideal of diversity: a kind of cult of the particular that shows itself in a wide range of contemporary social phenomena, from the increase of aggressive nationalism and tribalism around the globe to the increasing distrust of large-scale government in the United States. We can speculate about the underlying reasons why particular groups in virtually all societies of our world now tend to stress their differences from others rather than their commonalities, and to seek ways of enhancing and institutionalizing those differences rather than downplaying them: insecurity about religious and social identities in a world where modern communications constantly confuse and hybridize them; fear of forced ideological and political amalgamation on the heels of a century of totalitarian oppression; an intellectual discomfort with generalization and grand schemes of meaning manifesting itself in the doggedly particularizing mode of thought known as post-modernism. Whatever the motivating factors may be, particularity and diversity — being yourself, being different, and being seen as just as good as the members of other groups with whom you might be compared — is clearly a dominant pattern of contemporary social ambition.

All of this, certainly, is understandable as a political phenomenon, but the implications of this "cult of the particular" for the life of Christians seem more worrisome. The good news proclaimed in the writings of the New Testament, after all, is not simply the news that eternal life, founded on a new relationship of humanity with God, is now available to us as individuals through faith in Jesus as Lord. It is also, as Paul reminds us (Rom. 12:4-5; 1 Cor. 10:17; 12:12-13), that this new life forms us, many though we are, into a "single body." The Fourth Gospel depicts Jesus, at the decisive moment in his earthly mission on the night before his death, praying that the divine "glory" of his own eternally shared life with his Father may be realized and reflected now in an analogous unity of his disciples with him and with each other (John 17:1-5, 9-11, 20-23): "I in them and you in me, that they may become perfectly one, that the world may know that you have sent me" (17:23). The Letter to the Ephesians conceives of the divine "plan for the fullness of time" as including the reconciliation of Jews and Gentiles — people who have known the God of history and people who have not — in a single "household of God" (Eph. 2:19), a single "holy temple" (2:21), a single, fully human "body" (2:15-16) that is the first step in God's still larger plan "to unite all things in [Christ], things in heaven and things on earth" (1:10). The unity of Christian disciples, in these and other passages in the New Testament, is presented as a central aspect of salvation itself. This unity certainly contains and supports diversity, in the way a single healthy body maintains the diversity of its members, but it ultimately stands above all diversity as well.

As a result, Christian preaching and ministry, in order to be authentic, must always include a call to concrete and practical unity with other Christians as an integral part of its message of salvation. One of the main terms for this in the New Testament is, of course, κοινωνία — *communio,* a sharing of some material or spiritual reality that results in lived solidarity on the social and personal level. The earliest Christians in Jerusalem, St. Luke tells us in the second chapter of Acts, "devoted themselves to the apostles' teaching and to κοινωνία, to the breaking of bread and the prayers" (Acts 2:42); presumably their unity in faith, in prayer and in the action of the Eucharist all served as the elements of the "communion" or "fellowship" that characterized, in the most general sense, their religious life. Other New Testament passages use this same word to convey how the early Christians shared in each other's faith (Philem. 6), in the gospel (Phil. 1:5), in esteem and respect for the vocations of other disciples (Gal. 2:9), in the Holy Spirit (Phil. 2:1), or in the sufferings of Christ (Phil. 3:10; 1 Pet. 4:13), and to denote their sharing of material goods with the poor (Rom. 12:13; 15:26; 2 Cor. 8:4; 9:13; Phil. 4:15). The opening verses of the First Letter of John even suggest that the very purpose of preaching the gospel is to create a relationship of κοινωνία, of sharing or communion, that includes the hearers, the preachers, and God: "That which we have heard and seen we proclaim also to you, so that you may have *communion* with us; and our *communion* is with the Father and with his Son Jesus Christ" (1 John 1:3).

This last text suggests a second dimension or axis of church life that in the New Testament and throughout the history of the Christian churches seems inseparable from this "horizontal" dimension of mutual sharing among believers, and of their common share in the life of God: the "vertical" axis of witness or authority or leadership, rooted in the proclamation of the gospel by those who have already "heard and seen." Like the original disciples themselves, Christians always receive the news of salvation in Christ as a word from others: as preached in the community gathered for worship, as handed down by other believers in family or school or the wider culture, as suggested by a book, a film, or the word of a friend. And this intrinsic dependence on others for the communication of the gospel of God requires, in turn, some abiding structure within Christian communities for assuring the lively continuity of the word in all its fullness and integrity, a structure by which individuals within the community are empowered to proclaim the good news of salvation and judgment independently of the preferences and responses of their hearers — "in season and out of season" (2 Tim. 4:2) — to preserve and continue the tradition of preached faith established by the apostles.

Every human group or community, after all, needs structure and leadership if it is to last beyond its original moment of "togetherness." It needs people with the power to make decisions in the name of the group, to act as the community's memory, and to challenge the community to grow and change in a way consistent with its own identity. St. Thomas Aquinas, drawing on Aristotle's *Politics,* puts this sociological truism succinctly:

> Now a social life cannot exist among a number of people unless it is under the presidency of one to look after the common good; for many, as such, seek many things, whereas one attends only to one. Therefore the Philosopher says, at the beginning of the *Politics,* that wherever many things are directed to one [goal], we shall always find one at the head directing them.[1]

In Christian communities, such headship or authority is always exercised representatively. Jesus, as the incarnate Word of God, represents the Father in his human words and actions. One might even say he represents his own divine nature and person in his human flesh, as he works the healing and transformation of sinful humanity by his preaching and ministry. In the twentieth chapter of John, the risen Jesus is presented as giving this same representative mission to the Twelve, by pouring out the Holy Spirit upon them: "As the Father has sent me, so I send you. . . . Receive the Holy Spirit. If you forgive the sins of any, they are forgiven; if you retain the sins of any, they are retained" (John 20:21, 23). Within the community of faith, individuals commissioned in the power of the Holy Spirit to speak to human beings in the name of Christ exercise Christian headship, and speak to the Father, along with Christ, in the name of humanity. Since earliest Christianity, virtually every community of disciples — with the exception of a

---

1. *Summa Theologiae* I, 96.4 (trans. by the Fathers of the English Dominican Province [London, 1920], 1:489 [modified]), citing Aristotle, *Politics* I, 2 (1254a28).

few deliberately unstructured groups like the early Quakers — has ordained leaders to exercise this function of representative headship. Although the understanding of ordination and office has varied widely, it always consists of some form of authority to preach to the community and to lead it in prayer, to focus and unify the central and vital activities of the community of faith by speaking in the name of the tradition, of the Scriptures, and so of the apostles and Christ himself. For our inherent human diversity to be welded together into the communion in faith and service that constitutes the fulfillment of God's saving plan in history, some element of representative leadership or headship seems indispensable.

In recent years, the ancient notion of the church as fundamentally constituted by communion has reemerged as an important category for the theological self-understanding of many Christians. First promoted in this century by Orthodox thinkers such as Nicholas Afanasieff and, more recently, John Zizioulas, this approach to understanding the church was espoused by Roman Catholics such as Yves Congar in the 1950s, Joseph Ratzinger in the 1960s, and in recent years most extensively and powerfully by the Dominican theologian Jean-Marie Roger Tillard, in his works *Église d'églises* and *L'Église locale*.[2] The guiding image for this understanding of the church is that of the eucharistic assembly of the faithful, gathered around their bishop at the table of the Lord to hear the gospel proclaimed and to share — through the invocation of the Holy Spirit — in the sacramental gifts that make present Christ's unique offering of himself to the Father on the Cross. "Eucharistic" or *communio* ecclesiology recognizes in this community of faith and worship the full reality of what the creed calls the "one, holy, catholic and apostolic church," wholly present here and now in a sacramental way without being limited to, or exhaustively identified with, any particular community at any particular time and place. In the words of *Lumen Gentium*, the Second Vatican Council's constitution on the church:

"The church of Christ is truly present in all the lawful local congregations of the faithful which, united to their shepherds, are themselves

---

2. Jean-Marie Roger Tillard, O.P., *Église d'églises: L'ecclésiologie de communion* (Paris: Cerf, 1987); *L'Église locale* (Paris: Cerf, 1995). For a brief summary of modern "eucharistic ecclesiology" or "ecclesiology of communion," in the context of contemporary North American discussions between Orthodox and Catholic theologians, see my article "Headship and Communion: American Orthodox-Catholic Dialogue on Synodality and Primacy in the Church," *Pro Ecclesia* 5 (1996): 55-72.

called churches in the New Testament. For in their own locality these are the new people called by God, in the Holy Spirit and with full conviction. . . . In these communities, although frequently small and poor, or living in the diaspora, Christ is present, by whose power the one holy, catholic and apostolic church is gathered together."[3]

The universal church, which is realized and made concretely present through Christ in each of these local Eucharistic celebrations, is itself a much wider reality. For Roman Catholic theology, especially, it is only through explicit and intentional communion with the universal church, in its history of faith and worship reaching back to the apostles and in its present multicultural extension throughout the world, that a local church becomes the Catholic Church in a particular place and time. It is only by communion in faith, love, and Christian practice with all the other communities of apostolic faith and worship, in other words, that any particular community becomes an embodiment of the authentic church of Christ, which is sometimes described as "a communion of communions."

Although the concept of the church as communion was not, in fact, used often in the documents of Vatican II, it has been embraced with increasing frequency in official papal documents since then,[4] and "represents," in the words of Tillard, "the horizon against which the great statements [of the council] about the church and its mission become distinguishable."[5] It is highly significant, then, that in the language of its document on ecumenism, *Unitatis Redintegratio* (1965), that same council

3. *Lumen Gentium,* No. 26, in Norman P. Tanner, ed., *Decrees of the Ecumenical Councils* (London and Washington: Sheed and Ward/Georgetown, 1990), 2.870. The Council's document on the office of bishops, *Christus Dominus,* describes a diocese or "particular church" *(ecclesia particularis)* in similar terms, as an essentially Eucharistic community in which the one church is concretely encountered: "A diocese is a section of the people of God whose pastoral care is entrusted to a bishop in cooperation with his priests. Thus, in conjunction with their pastor and gathered by him into one flock in the Holy Spirit through the Gospel and the Eucharist, they constitute a particular church. In this church, the one, holy, catholic and apostolic Church of Christ is truly present and at work *(vere inest et operatur)."* *(Christus Dominus,* 11; Tanner 2.924).

4. See, for example, the Apostolic Constitution *Sacrae Disciplinae Leges* (1983), promulgating the new Code of Canon Law for the Roman Catholic Church; the Final Report of the Extraordinary Synod of Bishops gathered in Rome in 1985 to celebrate the twentieth anniversary of the close of Vatican II (Washington, 1986), p. 17; and Pope John Paul II's Apostolic Exhortation on the vocation of laypeople, *Christifideles Laici* (1988), p. 19.

5. *Église d'églises,* p. 9 (translation mine).

speaks of ecclesial communities other than the Catholic Church in terms of "separation from full communion," rather than in the more traditional terms of heresy or schism, and adds the affirmation that "those who believe in Christ and have been truly baptized are in some kind of communion with the Catholic Church *(in quadam cum ecclesia catholica communione)*, even though this communion is imperfect."[6] In the language of the ecclesiology of communion, which was just beginning to be developed in Catholic thought at the time of Vatican II, this statement is itself a way of recognizing the genuinely ecclesial character of other Christian bodies, which, as the document admits, "can exist outside the visible boundaries of the Catholic Church," possessing in themselves at least some of the gifts of grace which "properly belong to the one church of Christ."[7] Like the council's constitution on the church *Lumen Gentium,* which uses the analogy of the subsistence of the transcendent Word of God in the historical humanity of Jesus to speak of the "unique church of Christ" as "subsisting in" — but not exclusively limited to or circumscribed by — the Catholic Church,[8] this language marks the beginning of a new, more inclusive ecclesiology within the Church's official presentation of itself, an ecclesiology which is still in the early stages of its reception and theological development thirty-five years later.

My task here, however, is not to reflect on the developing use of the ecclesiology of communion in Catholic theology. It is to discuss the Petrine ministry, the ministry of the bishop of Rome filling the same role among all Christians that Peter in the New Testament received from the Lord, to be an instrument for preserving and building communion both within the Catholic family and among all communities of Christians.[9] My task, I assume, is also to reflect on this connection of Petrine ministry with ecclesial communion as a Roman Catholic, as a historical theologian concerned especially with the early church, and as a person who has been

6. *Unitatis Redintegratio,* No. 3 (Tanner 2.910).

7. *Unitatis Redintegratio,* No. 3 (Tanner 2.910).

8. *Lumen Gentium* 8 (Tanner 2.854). It is significant that both *Lumen Gentium* and *Unitatis Redintegratio* were promulgated on the same day, near the end of the Council's Third Session, November 21, 1964. They represent two expressions of a single, dramatically new direction in the Catholic Church's self-understanding.

9. On this theme, and on the subject of this paper more generally, see the recent collection of essays by theologians of many Christian churches: James F. Puglisi, ed., *Petrine Ministry and the Unity of the Church* (Collegeville, Minn.: Liturgical Press, 1999).

involved for twenty years in the dialogue between the Orthodox and Catholic communions in North America. What I can hope to write in the short space of this essay will perhaps not be new or comprehensive. Nevertheless, I hope it will be of some use to point out some of the main features of how this Petrine ministry of the Roman bishops — as distinct from their other episcopal functions — was understood in the centuries when the worldwide communion of all the Christian churches was still a functioning if fragile organism, and to reflect briefly on what lessons the papal ministry of the first millennium might offer us now, at the start of a third.

Peter's role in the writings of the New Testament is distinctive and well known. The first of the Twelve to be called, according to the synoptic Gospels, Peter acquires in all four Gospels the role of spokesperson and leader among them, and retains it in a distinctive way in Acts. In Matthew's Gospel, it is Peter's confession that Jesus is the Messiah that prompts Jesus both to recognize the divine origin of his act of faith (Matt. 16:17) and to promise to build an everlasting community, an ἐκκλησία, on "this rock," in which Peter, the "man of rock," will in some way have a decisive binding authority, "the keys of the Kingdom of heaven" (Matt. 16:18-19). Peter's portrait in the Gospels is a strikingly human one: ready to speak for the rest and to put hard questions to Jesus about the challenges of following him (e.g., Mark 10:28; Luke 12:41), rashly confident in his own ability to remain faithful in Jesus' final crisis (Mark 14:29-31), touchingly devoted to Jesus (John 21:15-17), and hesitant to allow Jesus to wash his feet in humble service (John 13:6-9). He embodies both the eager affection and commitment of the disciple and the weakness and cowardice of the sinner (e.g., Mark 14:37-41, 66-72). Yet Luke's Gospel depicts Jesus at the Last Supper giving Peter the commission to support the faith of his fellow disciples in the coming hour, when they are "scandalized" by his own failure, precisely because Peter himself will be one who has both fallen and returned to fidelity: "Simon, Simon, behold, Satan has demanded to have you all that he might sift you like wheat; but I have prayed for you [singular], that your faith may not fail. And when you have turned again, strengthen your brothers" (Luke 22:31-32). The twenty-first chapter of John's Gospel gives a more extensive account of Peter's commissioning. After Peter rushes to greet the risen Lord, Jesus feeds Peter and then questions him three times about his love for him. After Peter professes his love with great warmth, Jesus charges him to "feed [Jesus'] sheep," to act as shepherd of those who "hear his voice" and know him as their true shepherd (John 21:15-17; see John 10:1-18). Like Jesus himself, who as the true shepherd has "laid down his life for his sheep" (John 10:11, 17f.), Peter's commissioned role, in John 21, is to end in his being led to death as Jesus was, in his "glorifying God" as Jesus did, by the witness of his blood (John 21:18-19).

The New Testament writings, of course, say nothing directly about a continuing function of leadership like Peter's within the later community of disciples, and give no hint of a process for appointing successors to his role as "rock," "shepherd," and source of strength for the others. Rudolf Pesch has recently argued, however, that the portrait of Peter, when taken within the whole context of the New Testament, has an unmistakably symbolic character as delineating the type of what we have come to call "episcopal" leadership. Peter's depiction, Pesch says, is "ordered towards succession: the succession of a personal witness and mediator, who — precisely as successor — must take responsibility for the tradition and preserve the unity of the church."[10] In Matthew's Gospel and the double work of Luke, especially, Peter emerges as both taking the lead among the Twelve in speaking and proclaiming the news of Easter, and as representing their common vocation (compare, for example, Matt. 16:19 with 18:18; and see Acts 15:7-21), a role Cardinal Ratzinger has recently characterized as "a collegially supported, personal ultimate responsibility."[11]

Pesch even suggests that the selection and arrangement of the New Testament canon — a process that seems to have been of special concern in Rome in the late second century, especially if we date the Muratorian Fragment to that period[12] — reflects a clear concern with succession in roles of authority in the church. Beginning with a presentation of the figure of the Lord himself in the Gospels, the New Testament, as we now have

10. Rudolf Pesch, "Was an Petrus sichtbar war, ist in den Primat eingegangen," in *Il Primato del Successore di Pietro,* Atti del Simposio Teologico, Roma, Dicembre 1996 (Vatican City, 1998), p. 66 (translation mine); cf. pp. 72-82.

11. Joseph Cardinal Ratzinger, *Salz der Erde: Christentum und katholische Kirche an der Jahrtausendwende. Ein Gespräch mit Peter Seewald* (Stuttgart, 1996), p. 273, quoted by Pesch, p. 74 and n. 77.

12. See Bruce Metzger, *The Canon of the New Testament: Its Origin, Development and Significance* (Oxford, 1987), pp. 191-201, 305-307; for the view that it reflects a list of the canon from the latter half of the fourth century, see Lee M. McDonald, *The Formation of the Christian Biblical Canon* (Peabody, Mass.: Hendrickson, 1995), pp. 209-220.

it, moves on to portray the rapid development of the community of disciples, under the varied leadership of Peter, James and Paul, in the Book of Acts. Then, in the Pauline letters, we find a summary of Paul's own unique authoritative role as the apostle "born out of due time" (1 Cor. 15:8), as well as his authoritative "testament" in the Pastoral Letters. The Letter of James and the two letters attributed to Peter bring us back to the traditions of these apostles at Jerusalem and Rome, respectively, while the three Johannine letters show yet another early community — perhaps in Syria — expressing its understanding of ecclesial communion. Finally, the Book of Revelation returns us to the glorious portrait of the victorious Christ, in the dramatic final conflict between his "flock" and the hostile power of the pagan empire, focused in the city of Rome, capital of the political world and embodiment of resistance to the gospel.

Drawing on the work of a number of contemporary German scholars, Pesch observes:

> Traditions concerning Peter developed in a curiously scattered way in a variety of church settings, and are witnessed and handed on in those places; they reflect the authority of the first apostle throughout the church. . . . But we find traditions concerning Peter in a particular concentration and with striking density in Rome — something that has been too little noticed and appreciated. In all probability, Mark and Silas helped form there a "school of Peter." It is well known that the Roman community was most heavily involved in the development of the canon. And it was also extremely well prepared to do so, given its documentation.[13]

Pesch then goes on to list the New Testament writings that seem to have been associated with the Christian community at Rome: the Gospel of Mark; perhaps also Luke and Acts; the two Letters of Peter and the Second Letter to Timothy; as well as non-canonical First Letter of Clement, which is written from the church of Rome to the church of Corinth around the end of the first century and witnesses to the continuing authority of Peter and Paul in both churches.

"When the time came," concludes Pesch, "in which the community at Rome read all these documents — along with those added to them by the canon — as a unity, and when a single episcopal office had developed

13. Pesch, "Was an Petrus sichtbar war," pp. 84f.

from a more broadly conceived episcopacy, the church there could discover what had flowed from the traditions concerning Peter into its own primacy."[14]

The point Pesch is making here is a crucial one for our understanding of the development of whatever primacy among Christian leaders we associate with the later bishops of Rome. Acts and the Petrine Epistles make it clear that both Peter and Paul, whom the New Testament canon holds up as different, yet complementary, types of apostolic church founders, eventually made their way to the imperial capital and preached the gospel there (Acts 25:11-12; 28:14-31; 1 Pet 5:12-13). First Clement, written from the Roman community about 96, alludes to the two apostles' recent martyrdom as an example of faith,[15] and Ignatius of Antioch, writing to the Roman Church about 115, mentions their "commanding" apostolic authority there.[16] Eusebius of Caesaraea, in his *Ecclesiastical History*, quotes a certain Roman "churchman" named Gaius as claiming, about the year 200, that he could show any visitor to Rome the "monuments" to Peter and Paul, "who founded this church," in the Vatican cemetery and on the Ostian Way;[17] and the excavations carried out under the Vatican basilica in the 1940s confirm that Christians were venerating Peter's remains there, with great devotion, from at least the 160s. The witness of Peter and Paul to Christ in Rome, first with their preaching and finally with their blood, was clearly of crucial importance both to the authors of the New Testament books and to the churches which received those books as a normative canon, and seems to have been the main reason for the unique importance of the imperial capital to Christians all over the Roman world in the second and third centuries.

This witness to apostolic faith was not simply a matter of historical interest, let alone of pious nostalgia; it was the foundation of a publicly accessible standard for continuance in the faith of the founding generation of Christians. As the churches of the late second century faced their first serious doctrinal and disciplinary challenge in the esoteric traditions and anti-institutional practices of the groups we categorize as "Gnostic," writers like Irenaeus of Lyon and Tertullian of Carthage realized that the most

---

14. Pesch, "Was an Petrus sichtbar war," p. 86.
15. 1 Clement 5.
16. Ignatius, Rom 4.3.
17. Eusebius, *Ecclesiastical History*, 2.25.7.

reliable indicator and guarantee of "mainstream" Christian faith was continuity in the leadership of the communities which the apostles themselves had founded. Irenaeus argues this powerfully at the start of the third book of *Against the Heresies,* insisting that "the tradition which originates from the apostles . . . is preserved by means of the successions of elders in the churches."[18] Believers should be able to check the authenticity of contemporary preaching by consulting the traditions of churches with known pedigrees of apostolic leadership, but since such research would be a long and complicated task, Irenaeus writes, they do this

> . . . by indicating the apostolic tradition of that very great, very ancient, and universally known church founded and organized at Rome by the two most glorious apostles, Peter and Paul. . . . For to this church, on account of its more weighty priority *(propter potentiorem principalitatem),* every church — that is, the faithful from all over — must necessarily agree *(convenire),* for in it the tradition that comes from the apostles is preserved by those who come from all over."[19]

Although the meaning of several phrases in this celebrated passage is disputed, Irenaeus seems clearly to be representing the Christian community at Rome as both a depository for the apostolic tradition of faith and as a kind of communication center, a focal point for communion in that apostolic faith, for the churches throughout the world. The reason for the Roman community's *principalitas,* Irenaeus's argument here suggests, is not simply its age, nor its political prominence, but the "firstness" conferred on it by the final presence of Peter and Paul there, in life and in death. This "firstness" was "stronger" *(potior* or *potentior)* than that of other prominent early communities because of this apostolic association, and it therefore gave Rome a privileged position as a source of normative Christian teaching and practice.

Two further points are especially important to note in this oft-quoted early text. First, the "primacy" that Irenaeus acknowledges to exist in Rome is its primacy as a church among the other churches, not the primacy of its bishop among the other bishops. This point is important because it now seems indisputable that the office of bishop, along with those of presbyter and deacon, evolved only gradually during the first century or

18. *Against the Heresies,* 3.2.2; cf. Tertullian, *Prescription against Heretics,* p. 32.
19. *Against the Heresies,* 3.2.2.

so after the apostles' deaths. These offices probably reached their classical form at different times in different local churches. The Pastoral Letters, for instance, which may date from the last two decades of the first century, indicate a church or churches in which the terms ἐπίσκοπος ("bishop," "overseer," "supervisor") and πρεσβύτερος ("elder") are used interchangeably, and so suggest government by a body of elders rather than a single bishop. The same is true of 1 Clement, which probably was written in Rome about 96, and seems even to be the case in *The Shepherd of Hermas,* a collection of quasi-apocalyptic visions and instructions probably composed in the Roman church over several decades between 120 and 150. Although the letters of Ignatius of Antioch, dating from around 115, clearly witness to a church structure in Syria and Asia Minor in which headship is vested in a single bishop, supported by a body of presbyters and assisted in his work of ministry by deacons, this pattern may have evolved more slowly in the churches of the West. Scholars suggest that the danger of persecution, as well as the size of the city, may have forced early Christians in the city of Rome to continue meeting in some twenty small local gatherings or "house churches," each with its local leadership structure, rather than as a single eucharistic body under the headship of a single bishop, well into the middle of the second century.[20] Even after the development of the classical monepiscopal structure at Rome, probably by 150 at the latest, it remained customary until the late fourth century for writers to refer to the primacy of the Roman church as a primacy of its "seat" or "chair" (*sedes, cathedra*) — of its authority to teach, conceived impersonally — rather than of the holder of the chair. As Tillard has said of the Roman bishop in the early church, "His primacy came from his church, which in turn owed it to what the glorious witness of Peter and Paul had brought about in her. He had no personal authority apart form the prerogatives (*presbeia*) of his local church."[21]

Secondly, this passage by Irenaeus reflects what the communion of the churches actually meant to a bishop laboring to keep his congregation centered in the faith and life of the apostolic community. Beginning in the concrete sacramental experience of communion in the sacrificed body and blood of Christ at the local Eucharist, early Christians understood these

---

20. See James S. Jeffers, *Conflict at Rome: Social Order and Hierarchy in Early Christianity* (Minneapolis: Fortress, 1991), for a study of the question and further bibliography.

21. J.-M. R. Tillard, *The Bishop of Rome* (Wilmington: Michael Glazier, 1983), p. 86.

local communities, with their members, to be in a communion with one another that was grounded in shared faith, shared discipleship and witness, and shared participation in the divine sonship of Christ by the gift of the Holy Spirit. This wider communion was expressed in a variety of ways: by the exchange of letters between the churches, including reports on local problems and on the decisions of local synods; by hospitality shown to credentialed visiting Christians from other churches, both in the homes of the faithful and at the Eucharist; by the canonical requirement, from at least the third century on, that a bishop be ordained to his office not just by one, but by a number of bishops from neighboring churches;[22] and by the mutual profession of apostolic faith by the bishops of all the churches, expressed in letters issued by each at the time of his episcopal ordination, as well as by the collective witness of regional synods. The major churches of each province or region seem to have kept up-to-date records of what communities were known to profess this apostolic faith, and what bishops were known to stand in legitimate succession from apostolic origins. The touchstone for this recognition, especially in the Latin West, as well as the chief means of assuring communion with the worldwide body of churches, Irenaeus and later writers suggest, was for each local church to stand in publicly recognized communion of faith with the Church of Rome through its bishop.[23]

Cyprian of Carthage, for instance — always a tenacious and eloquent defender of the local bishop's normative role in grounding the unity of each church as a community of grace — wrote to a bishop named Florentius in 254 that the communion of bishops with one another is the "glue" that makes the "church which is catholic and one" a reality.[24] Yet Cyprian also alluded, in other passages, to the "chair of Peter" as "the first church, from

22. See Hippolytus, *Apostolic Tradition,* 2; Cyprian, Ep. 67.5.1; Council of Arles (314), can. 20 (if possible, seven neighboring bishops, but at least three); Council of Nicaea (325), can. 4 (if possible, all the bishops of a province, but at least three).

23. For a well-documented description of how communion actually worked, see the famous article of Ludwig Hertling, published in English translation by Jared Wicks as a monograph: *Communio: Church and Papacy in Early Christianity* (Chicago: Loyola University Press, 1972). See also Y. Congar, "La collégialité de l'épiscopat et la primauté de l'évêque de Rome dans l'histoire (Brève esquisse)," *Angelicum* 47 (1970): 403-27, esp. 404; Klaus Schatz, *Papal Primacy from its Origins to the Present* (Collegeville: Liturgical Press, 1996), pp. 17-21.

24. Ep. 66.8; cf. *De ecclesiae catholicae unitate,* 5.

which the unity of the episcopate has arisen,"[25] and acknowledged that to be in communion with the bishop of Rome is "to endorse firmly and to maintain both the unity and the charity of the catholic church."[26] Augustine, writing to other African bishops in the year 397, argued that the influence of the metropolitan bishops of Carthage — including Cyprian, presumably — had been maintained through the centuries, in the face of schism, by the fact that "he saw himself joined by letters of communion both to the Roman Church, in which the primacy of the apostolic throne (*apostolicae cathedrae principatus*) always flourished, and to other lands, from which the gospel came to Africa itself; and he was prepared to defend himself before these churches, if his enemies tried to alienate them from him."[27] Internal cohesion, stability in the profession of faith, and communion with "the churches overseas" were intrinsically linked in the minds of most early Christian writers in the orthodox tradition from the second century onward.

Many aspects of the life and structure of early Christian communities began to change radically after the Emperor Constantine, probably in the year 313, granted official toleration to all religions and began to show special favor toward and interest in Christianity. Churches grew, acquired wealth, and built new and splendid public buildings for their assemblies, supported by imperial donations. Bishops became magistrates, traveled at the public expense, and lauded and advised the emperor. Constantine himself — although not baptized until a few weeks before his death — took on the role of promoter of unity among Christians, even on matters of faith, when their disputes threatened to rupture civil *concordia*,[28] and reportedly described himself as the bishop "ordained by God to supervise (ἐπισκοπεῖν) those outside the Church."[29]

---

25. Ep. 59.14.

26. Ep. 48.3; cf. Ep. 55.1. Here and elsewhere in the Latin Patristic tradition of the first four centuries, "charity" (*caritas*) seems to have a more concrete, ecclesial meaning than simply that of mutual affection or the divine gift of love; in Cyprian's letters, especially, it often seems to be used to describe ecclesial communion itself. See my article, "Structures of Charity: Bishops' Gatherings and the See of Rome in the Early Church," in Thomas J. Reese, ed., *Episcopal conferences: Historical, Canonical and Theological Studies* (Washington: Georgetown University Press, 1989), pp. 25-58, esp. pp. 53-55.

27. Ep. 43.7.

28. See his letter to Alexander of Alexandria and Arius in Eusebius, *Life of Constantine* 2.63-72; also Opitz, *Athanasius Werke* III/1 (Urkunden zur Geschichte des Arianischen Streites 27), pp. 58-62.

29. Eusebius, *Life of Constantine* 4.24. See Johannes Straub, "Kaiser Konstantin als

In this new world, the bishops of Rome also began to conceive of and exercise their role of presiding over Peter's church, in Peter's "chair," in at least two new and significant ways. First, by the time of Pope Damasus in the 370s, they themselves began to adopt the curial style of Roman emperors and provincial governors in their official correspondence, issuing rescripts in response to disciplinary or doctrinal inquiries from bishops — even bishops outside of Italy — and claiming for themselves the right both to be the final instance of review for the legislation and appointments of other churches and the final court of appeal for disputes among bishops.[30] Pope Innocent I articulated this new understanding of the authority of the Roman bishop's office in 417 in a reply to a letter from a provincial synod in Carthage that had asked him to join them in condemning the errors of Pelagius and his followers. Innocent interprets their request (which was probably due, at least in part, to the continuing polemics of Pelagius's supporters against Augustine in Rome and other parts of Italy) as an acknowledgment of his own role as ultimate judge in central questions of doctrine. So he writes:

> You have, by your priestly office, preserved the institutions of the fathers, and have not spurned that which they decreed by a sentence not human but divine: that whatever is done, even though it be in distant provinces, should not be ended until it comes to the knowledge of this see, that by its authority the whole just pronouncement should be strengthened, and that from there the other churches, like waters proceeding from their original sources and flowing through the different regions of the world — pure streams from an incorrupt head — should assimilate what they ought to enjoin, whom they ought to wash, and

---

ἐπίσκοπος τῶν ἐκτός," *Studia Patristica* 1 (= Texte und Untersuchungen 63: Berlin, 1957): 678-695; Raffaello Farina, "ἐπίσκοπος τῶν ἐκτός (Eusebio, *De vita Const.* IV, 24)," *Salesianum* 29 (1967): 409-413.

30. See, e.g., Pope Siricius, Ep. 1.20 (PL 13.1132); Pope Innocent I, Ep. 25.2 (PL 20.552). For further documentation, see my article, "Structures of Charity" (above, n. 25), p. 39; Roland Minnerath, "La tradition doctrinale de la primauté Pétrinienne au premier millénaire," *Il Primato des Successore di Pietro*, pp. 128-129. The principle that the bishops of Rome should act as the final court of appeal in disputes among bishops, not deciding the issue themselves but appointing a panel of bishops in the region to hear the case, was first enacted in canon 3 of the Synod of Serdica (343), in the context of the appeals of Athanasius and other Eastern bishops against the decisions of pro-Arian emperors; see Hamilton Hess, *The Canons of the Council of Sardica* (Oxford, 1958).

whom that water, worthy of pure bodies, should avoid as defiled with uncleansable filth.[31]

Similar strong assertions of the active authority of the Roman bishop, not only giving him a final say (never fully defined) in disciplinary and doctrinal disputes but even suggesting that all episcopal authority in the individual churches in some way flows from his, appear with some frequency in the letters of the fifth-century popes, especially in those addressed to bishops in the Latin West.[32] A number of them, for instance, spoke of the Roman church, or even of themselves personally, as the "head" of a universal body in which other churches are "members."[33] What was new was both the juridical style and centralizing ecclesial vision of these statements, and the gradual shift of emphasis from the institutional responsibilities and prerogatives of the Church over which, or the "seat" from which, the bishop of Rome presided, to those of his own person.

This leads us to the second new emphasis in the papacy's self-understanding during the fourth and fifth centuries: a striking tendency of most of the popes from Damasus on to identify themselves personally, almost mystically, with Peter himself. The practice was not simply a rhetorical convention; it seems to have been suggested, in part at least, by the traditional Roman understanding of inheritance, in which those who succeeded to property or to the headship of an extended family were actually

31. Innocent I, Ep. 29 (*PL* 33.780); tr. E. Giles, *Documents Illustrating Papal Authority, A.D. 96-454* (London: SPCK, 1952), p. 201.

32. For a full discussion of these sources, see M. Maccarrone, *La dottrina del primato papale dal IV all'VIII secolo nelle relazioni con le chiese occidentali* (Spoleto, 1960), pp. 56-75; see also, by the same author, *Apostolicità, episcopato e primato di Pietro: Ricerche e testimonianze dal II al V secolo* (= *Lateranum* 42/2 [1976]), pp. 214-285; *Romana Ecclesia Cathedra Petri* I (Rome: Herder, 1991), pp. 1-101.

33. This use of the Pauline body metaphor to characterize the role of the Roman church and bishop in the wider Christian community first appears in a letter written by Ambrose of Milan in 381, in the name of a synod of Italian bishops at Aquileia, to Emperors Gratian and Valentinian II, in the West, and Theodosius I, in the East. Ambrose asks the emperors to take measures to restore church unity; it is a body, he writes, scattered over the whole world, and its head is the *Romana ecclesia*. The same image, applied directly to the papal office, appears in Pope Siricius's response to Himerius of Tarracona, February 11, 385 (Ep. 1.20: *PL* 13.1146); in Pope Anastasius I's letter to Bishop John of Jerusalem, on the Origenist controversy of 400-401 (PL 20.68); and in Pope Celestine I's letter to the clergy of Constantinople, August 10, 430, at the height of the Nestorian crisis (ACO I, 1.1.84.2-4).

understood as representing, even impersonating, their ancestors.[34] The bishops of Rome, presiding as successor to the "first" of the apostles in the place where the bones of the two chief founding apostles lay buried, now came to see themselves as receiving Peter's promises from the Lord, carrying on Peter's witness, and taking up Peter's continuing pastoral concern for the Lord's people. "In view of our office," Pope Siricius wrote to Bishop Himerius of Tarragona in 385, "we are not free to dissemble or to keep silent, for our zeal for the Christian religion ought to be greater than anyone's. We bear the burdens of all who are heavy laden, or rather the blessed apostle Peter bears them in us, who in all things, we trust, protects and defends those who are heirs of his government."[35] "Peter watches with his eyes in what manner you exercise your office," wrote Pope Boniface I to his legate in Thessalonica in 419, because "he was appointed shepherd of the Lord's sheep in perpetuity."[36] Even the celebrated image of the "rock," in Jesus' words to Peter in Matthew 16:18 — taken by Cyprian as conveying a promise to all bishops[37] and by Augustine variously as referring to Christ, to Peter in person, or to Peter's faith[38] — came to be interpreted consistently by the Roman bishops, from at least the time of Damasus in the late fourth century, as the foundational text of their primacy, signifying the evangelical and pastoral authority of both Peter and his successors.[39] So, in the 440s, in one of his annual sermons on the anniversary of his episcopal election, Pope Leo the Great said boldly:

34. See Josef Fellermayr, *Tradition und Sukzession im Lichte des römisch-antiken Erbdenkens* (Munich: Minerva, 1979), pp. 347-416.

35. Ep. 1 (PL 13.1132), trans. Giles, *Documents Illustrating Papal Authority*, p. 142.

36. Ep. 5.1 (PL 20.762), trans. Giles, *Documents Illustrating Papal Authority*, p. 229.

37. E.g., Ep. 33.1.

38. Augustine sometimes takes the "rock" to refer to Christ (*In Joh Ev Tr* 124.5), sometimes to Peter's faith (*Ep ad Cath de sect. Don* 21.60; *In Ep Joh Tr* 10.1), once even to the Church (*In Joh Ev Tr* 7.14) — although this last passage does not refer directly to Matthew 16:18, but simply asserts that Peter is given his name because he represents the Church. In several sermons (76.1; 244.1; 270.2; 295.1) and in *Retr* 1.20.2, Augustine invites each hearer to make up his or her own mind how to interpret the figure.

39. See the letter of the Roman synod of 382, arguing that the primacy of the "holy Roman church" within the worldwide communion of churches — in contrast to the newly proclaimed "second" rank of Constantinople — is founded on this text, not on any conciliar or secular decrees (PL 13.374). The contemporary African anti-Donatist bishop, Optatus of Milevis, also emphasized that the "keys" mentioned in Matthew 16:16-19 were given to Peter alone. *De schismate Donatistorum* 2.4; 7.3 [Books 1-6: c. 365; Book 7: c. 385].

There is a further reason for our celebration: not only the apostolic but also the episcopal dignity of the most blessed Peter, who does not cease to preside over his see and has obtained an abiding partnership with the eternal Priest. For the stability which the rock himself was given by that Rock, Christ, he conveyed also to his successors, and wherever any steadfastness is apparent, there without doubt is to be seen the strength of the shepherd.[40]

Behind these changes in papal language and style from the mid-fourth century on, however, one can detect in the sources significant differences in the way the bishops of Rome acted and spoke in different parts of the now-Christian empire. Since Batiffol, it has been customary to distinguish three quite separate "spheres of influence" for papal ministry, in which the popes tended to understand and assert their Petrine role in noticeably different ways.[41] Understandably, their strongest claim to authority in churches other than Rome itself was on the Italian peninsula, especially south of the Apennines, and in Sicily, Sardinia, Corsica and the smaller Tyrrhenian islands. This region, labeled by the historian Rufinus of Aquileia the *suburbicariae ecclesiae*,[42] paralleled the larger, supra-metropolitan or supra-provincial areas of the eastern Mediterranean world in which the bishops of Alexandria and Antioch, according to Canon 6 of the Council of Nicaea, and later those of Jerusalem and Constantinople as well, were recognized to have an extended influence. In the case of all of these ancient sees, the bishops were accorded an authority in adjacent provinces less formal and less frequently exercised than that of the metropolitan bishops of the provinces, but still real, based on the apostolic foundation — in the case of Constantinople, one laboriously constructed in the seventh century[43] — of these churches, and forming the basis of the Byzantine notion of the five great patriarchates or "pentarchy,"

40. Tr 5.4 (trans. Giles, pp. 281-282).
41. The best summary of these "spheres of influence," with full documentation, is still Pierre Batiffol, *Cathedra Petri* (Paris: Cerf, 1938), esp. pp. 41-79; see also C. Vogel, "Unité de l'église et pluralité des formes historiques d'organisation ecclésiastique du IIIe au Ve siècle," in Y. Congar and B. D. Dupuy, eds., *L'Épiscopat et l'église universelle* (Paris: Cerf, 1964), pp. 617-636. See also my article, "Structures of Charity," pp. 37-44.
42. *Church History* 10.6.
43. See Francis Dvornik, *The Idea of Apostolicity in Byzantium and the Legend of the Apostle Andrew*, Dumbarton Oaks Studies 4 (Cambridge, Mass.: Harvard University Press, 1958).

which was given its first legal status by the Emperor Justinian.[44] Although the bishops of "Old Rome" never claimed the title of "patriarch of the West" in antiquity, its basis lay in this canonical arrangement from the time of the great councils.

A wider, less clearly defined sphere in which the Bishops of Rome claimed influence in late antiquity was the whole western part of the Roman Empire: Europe west of the Rhine and south of the Danube, North Africa west of the Libyan desert, and the Balkans west of Thessalonica — with the exception of Greece, the Latin-speaking part of the ancient world. Even in the third century, the bishops of Rome were acknowledged to have the right and even the responsibility to intervene in church disputes in Spain and Gaul that could not be solved locally.[45] By the time of Augustine, although the bishops of Roman Africa were still fiercely proud of their ecclesial independence and regional cohesion, and still sensitive to every suggestion of Roman authoritarianism, they were increasingly ready to refer difficult doctrinal and even disciplinary disputes to be judged or confirmed by papal authority.[46] To secure their influence in these more distant areas, the popes resorted more and more to the practice of designating one local metropolitan bishop in each region as their personal legate or vicar; the bishop of Thessalonica was papal vicar in Thrace continually from the time of Pope Siricius (385), Pope Simplicius appointed the bishop of Seville his vicar in Spain in the 470s, and at least two attempts were made, in the fifth and sixth centuries, to confirm the same role in southern Gaul for the bishops of Arles. These vicars were not to usurp the functions of local metropolitans or synods, but simply to make sure, in the pope's name, that synods and episcopal elections were being held regularly

---

44. On the συμφωνία or "pentarchy" of patriarchal sees, see Justinian, Novellae 109 and 123; *Codex Iuris Civilis* III, 518-519; also Theodore of Studios, Ep. 124 (PG 99.1417C). See also Dvornik, *The Idea of Apostolicity*, pp. 163, 168, 235-237, 275-277. For a modern consideration of the theory of pentarchy from a Catholic perspective, see Ferdinand R. Gahbauer, *Die Pentarchietheorie: Ein Modell der Kirchenleitung von den Anfängen bis zur Gegenwart* (Frankfurt: Knecht, 1993).

45. See Cyprian, Ep. 59.9; 67.6; 68.

46. For a survey of the relations of the African church with the papacy, see J. E. Merdinger, *Rome and the African Church in the Time of Augustine* (New Haven: Yale University Press, 1997), esp. pp. 205-206; see also W. Marschall, *Karthago und Rom: Die Stellung der nordafrikanischen Kirche zum apostolischen Stuhl in Rom*, Päpste und Papsttum 1 (Stuttgart, 1971).

in an orderly way, that the traditional canons of church discipline were being observed, and that the apostolic faith was being maintained.[47]

The widest sphere of the exercise of papal authority in late antiquity, the sphere in which their claim to and their exercise of primacy was most vaguely defined, was the universal family of churches, including the Syriac- and Greek-speaking East of the Empire.[48] One kind of evidence for the claim to such wider primatial power was the willingness of a number of popes in the fourth and fifth centuries to intervene with imperial authorities on behalf of Greek bishops whom they considered orthodox, and who had been unjustly deprived of their sees. Julius I argued on behalf of the exiled Athanasius, in 340, that the bishop of another church of apostolic rank should not be deprived of his office without the consent of all the bishops, and that the canons gave Rome the right to be first judge in such cases.[49] John Chrysostom appealed to Pope Innocent I for support in 404, when he was under attack from enemies at court and from Patriarch Theophilus of Alexandria, and the pope protested vigorously both to Theophilus and to the emperor.[50] In the turbulent years just before the Council of Chalcedon, three major Eastern bishops who had been deposed at the "Robber Synod" of Ephesus in 449 — Eusebius of Dorylaeum, Flavian of Constantinople, and Theodoret of Cyrus — appealed to Pope Leo to overturn that decision by a judgment of his Roman synod, and in their letters explicitly recognized his "apostolic authority" to do so as Peter's successor.[51] Eusebius of Dorylaeum spelled out the reason for his appeal in terms both of the Roman see's continuance in the apostolic faith — the point Irenaeus had emphasized — and of the bishop of Rome's traditional concern for ecclesial communion:

> In the past and from the beginning, the Apostolic Throne has been accustomed to defend those who suffer evil, and to help those who have

47. See, for instance, Leo the Great, Ep. 6.5 and Ep. 14.12 to Anastasius, his vicar in Thessalonica. In the latter letter, he rebukes Anastasius sharply for failing to observe what we would call the principle of subsidiarity.

48. On the development and meaning of the notion of a "primacy of honor" for the Roman bishops, see my article "Position and Patronage in the Early Church: the Original Meaning of 'Primacy of Honour'," *Journal of Theological Studies* 44 (1993): 529-553.

49. Athanasius, *Apology against the Arians* 35; cf. Sozomen, *Church History* 3.10.1.

50. Innocent, Epp. 5 and 7 (PL 20.493-496; 501-508).

51. See ACO II, 2.1.77.9-11 (Flavian); SChr 111: 64.5-7, 22-24 (Theodoret); ACO II, 2.1.79.20-25 (Eusebius).

fallen among inescapable disputes. . . . The reason is that you hold to the right path and preserve your faith in our Lord Jesus Christ unshaken, and also that you show an undisguised charity towards all the brothers and sisters, all who have been called in the name of Christ.[52]

As part of a long-standing dispute with successive bishops of Constantinople over their use of the title, "ecumenical patriarch" — a title which the pope strongly believed no bishop in the Church should claim, since neither Peter nor Leo had done so[53] — Gregory the Great, in 599, warned the bishops of Illyricum, who had been summoned to a synod at Constantinople partly to support the patriarch's claim to that title, that nothing enacted in such a synod would be valid without the approval of the Apostolic See.[54] Gregory maintained his predecessors' high claims to the authority of the Roman bishop to intervene, when necessary, in the affairs of all the churches, for the sake of the gospel; yet he chose to style himself, with monastic humility, by the title "Servant of the Servants of God." In one letter, Gregory even suggested to Eulogius, the patriarch of Alexandria, that the bishops of all three of the ancient sees that claimed some connection with the apostle Peter — Antioch, Alexandria, and Rome — shared a single *principatus,* a single primatial authority, based on Christ's commission to "the first of the apostles."

Since, then, it is the one seat of one man, in which — by divine authority — three bishops now preside, whatever good I hear of you, I impute to myself; and whatever good you believe of me, impute it to your own deserts, since we are both "in" him, who says: "That all may be one, as you, Father, are in me and I am in you, that they, too, may be one in us."[55]

52. See n. 50.
53. Reg. 5.37.
54. Reg. 9.156.
55. Reg. 7.37 (July 597). Johannes Modesto, *Gregor der Grosse: Nachfolger Petri und Universalprimat* (St. Ottilien: EOS Verlag, 1989), p. 198, observes that the theory of a triply shared Petrine primacy, far from being a political maneuver as some have suggested, "fügt sich problemlos in den kollegial-episkopalen Gedanken Gregors ein." The notion of three Petrine sees is found already in what is probably a fourth-century part of the *Decretum Gelasianum* (3.3), although it is not interpreted there in the direction of a continuing shared Petrine ministry. Pope Leo, too, reminded Patriarch Maximus of Antioch, in the aftermath of the Council of Chalcedon (June 453), that Peter, as chief apostle, had preached one single

It is in their relationship to the general or ecumenical councils, summoned by the Christian emperors in times of great doctrinal dispute, however, that the ancient popes' nuanced sense of their own role in promoting the universal communion of the churches can best be seen. This relationship underwent a perceptible, if somewhat uneven, development between the time of Constantine and that of the seventh ecumenical council in 787. Papal involvement in the Council of Nicaea (325) and the First Council of Constantinople (381) was minimal, essentially a matter of reception of their canons and credal formulae after the event. At the abortive Council of Ephesus (431), Pope Celestine's legates joined in the anti-Nestorian sessions held under the presidency of Cyril of Alexandria, and were received with a great deal of respect; the letter from Celestine, which they read to the assembled bishops, exhorted them, in the name of all the apostles, to take seriously their "responsibility to guard the teaching committed to us by the just claim of our inheritance. . . . For to a teacher, the office of keeping safe what is committed to one's trust is not less dignified than that of promoting it."[56]

At Chalcedon, Pope Leo's role was a far more active one, both in the exchanges of letters that preceded and followed the council and in the proceedings themselves, through the involvement of his legates. Leo's own attitude toward synods and councils emerges clearly in many of his letters written during the Chalcedonian controversy. All official gatherings of bishops he considered to be under the guidance of the Holy Spirit, who leads the church into the fullness of truth.[57] But while the main role of local and provincial synods, in his view, was to regulate discipline and promote the peace and unity of the local church, the great universal councils

message throughout the world, "but with special teaching authority in the cities of Antioch and Rome" (Ep. 119.2); similarly, he demanded agreement in both doctrine and liturgical practice from Dioscorus of Alexandria as early as 445, because the Roman church still remained "in the teaching" of Peter, and it was unthinkable that his disciple Mark would deviate from his master's doctrine (Ep. 9.1). On Gregory's ascetical vision of authority, see Carole Straw, *Gregory the Great: Perfection in Imperfection* (Berkeley: University of California Press, 1988), pp. 66-106; Conrad Leyser, "Expertise and Authority in Gregory the Great: the Social function of *Peritia*," in John C. Cavadini, ed., *Gregory the Great: A Symposium* (Notre Dame, 1995), pp. 38-61.

56. ACO I, 1.3.55.19–56.1.

57. E.g., Ep. 166.1 (on a Roman synod); cf. John 16.10. On Leo's understanding of councils, see Hermann Josef Sieben, *Das Konzilsidee in der alten Kirche* (Paderborn: Schöningh, 1979), pp. 102-147; see also my "Structures of Charity," pp. 50-52.

had a higher goal: to formulate Christian teaching with a clarity beyond dispute, and to lay down rules for ecclesial practice that would have "perennial validity."[58] So in urging the Emperor Leo in 458, two years before his own death, to resist all efforts to persuade him to reopen the christological issue decided at Chalcedon, Leo insists that after a dispute such as this has been resolved in the proper canonical way, "to wish still to wrangle is the sign not of a peacemaking, but of a rebellious spirit." Chalcedon met what the pope implies are the two main criteria for any universal council's legitimacy: it was "attended by all the provinces of the Roman world and obtained universal acceptance for its decisions." It represented, in other words, a geographically ecumenical consensus of the churches, "and it is in complete harmony with the most sacred council of Nicaea"; its doctrine is also "historically ecumenical," in that it is consistent with the longer tradition.[59]

Hermann Josef Sieben, in his great history of the theology of councils, has argued that this same complementarity of spatially "horizontal" consensus and temporally "vertical" or historical continuity of faith also characterizes Leo's understanding of the relationship of the pope and the bishops at such a council. The bishops' role, in Leo's view, is to define and specify normative tradition in binding form, in language appropriate to the disputes of the day, by their own agreed formulation of the truth of the gospel. The pope's role, on the other hand, as he suggests in a number of letters, is not so much to propose final definitions of faith as to proclaim the long tradition, "to make clear what you already understand and to preach what you already believe"[60] — to provide, in other words, living contact with the church's memory by representing the voice and legacy of Peter. Even his own *Tome,* written to Patriarch Flavian of Constantinople at the height of the controversy over the constitution of Christ's person in the late 440s, is referred to in Leo's later letters as a work of "expounding," "explaining," "preaching," but not as being in itself a final resolution of the issues; he has written it, he tells his legate Julian of Kios, so that Patri-

58. Ep. 157.1, referring to Chalcedon. In Ep. 106.4, he insists — against the jurisdictional innovation of can. 28 of Chalcedon — that the canons of Nicaea (one of which this canon effectively replaces) were "laws destined to remain until the end of the world."

59. Ep. 164.2-3.

60. Ep. 165.1 (to the Emperor Leo); cf. Ep. 89 (to the Emperor Marcian); Tract. 25.2 (Christmas, 444). And see Sieben, pp. 123-128. For Leo's use of the language of "definition" for his own teaching role, see the passage from Ep. 120 quoted in the following note.

arch Flavian and all the other bishops "may know about the ancient and unique faith . . . , what we hold as handed down from God and what we preach without alteration."[61] So he writes to a local synod meeting at Chalcedon, two years after the council, that by reading all of his letters, "your holinesses may recognize that I am, with our God's help, the guardian both of the catholic faith and of the legislation of our ancestors."[62] Petrine authority, for Leo, outside the limits of his own episcopal and provincial sphere, is above all the authority of Peter the preacher, continuing to witness through Leo, his heir, to the Church's most ancient and authentic tradition.[63]

Stephan Otto Horn recently pointed out that the last two of the ancient councils usually recognized as "ecumenical" or definitive for Christian orthodoxy — the Third Council of Constantinople in 680-681 and the Second Council of Nicaea in 787 — both reveal, in the dialectic of communication between the pope and the (mainly Eastern) bishops in council, the same structure of authoritative teaching or proclamation of the tradition articulated for the council beforehand by the pope, and definitive confirmation by the consensus of bishops, after careful examination of the corroborative documentation from the theological and dogmatic tradition that had been assembled to support the papal position.[64] A

61. Ep. 34.2 (449). Cf. Ep. 89, written to the Emperor Marcian just before the council: the controversy is "about the Catholic faith, which we have learned through the holy fathers from the blessed Apostles, as the Spirit of God has instructed us, and which we teach." Cf. also Tract. 25.2; 62.2. In a letter written to Theodoret of Cyrus in June of 453, on the other hand, Leo reverses this line of thought and explains the work of the Council of Chalcedon as a matter of confirming his own teaching: he praises the Lord, "who has allowed us to sustain no harm in our brethren [at the council], but has corroborated, by the irrevocable assent of the whole brotherhood, what he had before *defined by our ministry,* to show that what had before been enacted by the first see of all, and received by the judgment of the whole Christian world, had truly proceeded from himself" (Ep. 120; tr. Giles, p. 314).

62. Ep. 114.2.

63. The recent joint statement of the Anglican–Roman Catholic International Commission (ARCIC), *The Gift of Authority,* refers to this episcopal and primatial task as "the ministry of memory" (30, 42).

64. Stephan Otto Horn, "Das Verhältnis von Primat und Episkopat im Ersten Jahrtausend: Eine geschichtlich-theologische Synthese," *Il Primato del Successore di Pietro,* pp. 194-213. For Constantinople III, see especially P. Conte, "Il significato del primato papale nei padri del VI concilio ecumenico," *Archivum historiae pontificiae* 15 (1977): 7-111. For Nicaea II, see Jean Gouillard, "L'Église d'Orient et la primauté romaine au temps de l'iconoclasme," *Istina* 21 (1976): 25-54; Vittorio Peri, "La Synergie entre le Pape et le Concile

year before the Third Council of Constantinople was formally convened, for instance, Pope Agatho and his local synod wrote a long expository letter to the participating bishops, presenting the Roman position on the two natural wills and activities of Christ, which had been formulated at the Lateran Synod of 649, as representing the continuous apostolic tradition of the church.[65] Agatho expresses here the expectation that the council will study his exposition, along with the corroborating evidence from earlier tradition he has provided, and confirm it as expressing the orthodox faith.

Likewise, Pope Hadrian I wrote to the Emperor Constantine IV and the Empress Irene shortly before the beginning of the Second Council of Nicaea in 787, laying out his understanding of the church's long practice of venerating religious images as something rooted in the apostolic faith in the Incarnate Word.[66] Hadrian wrote a similar letter to Tarasius, the patriarch of Constantinople, who had collaborated with the emperor in summoning the council, commending him for his orthodox faith and offering him "advice *(consilium)*" for the coming council, "so that your holiness might preserve the orthodox faith immutable, in both your preaching and your teaching."[67] After the council, Tarasius wrote in the name of the assembly to Pope Hadrian, assuring him that his letter had been read as the first item on the agenda, and that through him Christ had "prepared the food" the council had needed for its nourishment.[68] During the gathering itself, one of the first arguments made against the authority of the Synod of Hieria of 754, which had banned all images from churches and public places in the empire, was that it had not only excluded the representatives from the Roman church and disregarded the encyclical letter of the pope, "which the law requires for councils (καθὼς νόμος ἐστὶ τοῖς συνόδοις)," but had also excluded the representatives of the "apostolic" or patriarchal

oecuménique: Note d'histoire sur l'ecclésiologie traditionelle de l'Église indivise," *Irénikon* 56 (1983): 163-193; Emmanuel Lanne, "Rome et Nicée II," in F. Boespflug and N. Lossky, eds., *Nicée II, 787-1987* (Paris: Cerf, 1987), pp. 219-228.

65. Mansi XI, 234-286.
66. Mansi XII, 1055-1071.
67. Mansi XII, 1077-1084; see 1080D. Tarasius responded by recognizing Hadrian as successor to both Peter and Paul, and affirming that after studying the Scriptures himself and analyzing their teaching logically (συλλογιστικῶς), he receives Hadrian's teaching as representing the Catholic tradition "in fine fashion (εὖ καὶ καλῶς)." Clearly neither bishop is unaware of the ecclesiological implications of their alliance on the subject of the veneration of images, and they express themselves carefully.
68. Mansi XII, 458-460; see 459D.

churches of Antioch, Alexandria and Jerusalem, and had failed to seek their advice.[69] The examination and discussion of testimonies from the church fathers, appended to the Roman letters of doctrinal exposition, clearly played a crucial role in the proceedings of these ancient councils; however, before the beginning of each, the pope himself made a point of holding up to the council the longer tradition of the Church's faith in Christ, and of voicing his own sense of responsibility to "advise" both emperor and patriarch in Byzantium on the necessary conditions for remaining within the catholic communion.

How should we summarize the position and role of the bishops of Rome during the first millennium, a position that both they and the vast majority of bishops throughout the Christian world then accepted as sharing central characteristics with that of Peter among the apostles? Like Peter in the gospels, the heart of the Roman bishop's role in worldwide Christendom was to articulate the faith in Jesus as divine savior that bound the whole communion together. Like Peter's, too, this witness was often given in opposition to the ideals and interests of civil society, a μαρτυρία that marked off the Christian communion from the "human city," even after that city had become largely Christian in name and style. Although some early popes surely benefited from imperial patronage after the ascent of Constantine, others, like Julius and Leo and Gregory, found themselves in serious tension with the emperors, and some — like Vigilius, confined in house arrest until he accepted the canons of Constantinople II, or Martin I, exiled and mistreated to death by imperial order in 651 for articulating the christological faith — experienced something close to what we now call martyrdom. In itself, the growth of a self-consciously independent and universal ministry of leadership by the bishops of Rome laid the remote groundwork for our modern idea of the separation of church and state, of the radical difference between the ethnic and political and cultural community, on the one hand, and the community of Christian disciples on the other. Sometimes the bishops of Rome, in the centuries after Constantine, were figures of international stature, like Damasus, Leo, Gelasius and Gregory; some of them were obscure figures, like most of the popes of the sev-

69. Mansi XIII, 208E1-209A6. Pope Hadrian's letter to the emperor and empress listed all the unheeded attempts of his predecessors to persuade the Byzantine emperors and patriarchs to reestablish the veneration of images: Mansi XII, 1061A3-D6 (Latin text); 1059D10-1062B13 (Greek text).

enth century; some were blundering and incompetent, like Zosimus in Augustine's day, or Honorius two centuries later. Some of them were ambitious and authoritarian, like Stephen in the mid-third century, or Siricius and Innocent at the turn of the fifth, while others — notably Gregory the Great — gave a striking example of humility and the collegial spirit in the exercise of their primatial office. As Dom Emmanuel Lanne has recently pointed out, none of these popes ever exercised or imagined episcopal and papal authority apart from regularly functioning synodal structures, and much of their energy went into assuring that the local synods of Italy met regularly, followed the accepted canons, and accomplished the work they alone could do.[70] Popes in the early Church, with all their human variations in virtue, intelligence, and historical opportunity, seem, in fact, to have continued to do what Peter was commissioned to do in the Gospels: not necessarily to be autocrats, oracles, or even heroes, but to keep alive the central tradition of faith in Christ and to "strengthen the brethren," to promote continuing Christian communion in spite of, and sometimes in full consciousness of, their own weakness.

Applied to our own time, with all its bewildering possibilities for discontinuity, individualism and destructive competition hidden under the guise of a healthy, cultivated diversity, this sketchy summary of the early Petrine ministry of the bishops of Rome suggests, it seems to me, at least a few possible lessons:

First, papal primacy really is about promoting the unity and continuity of all the Christian communities in faith, life, and worship. It is about communion. It is not primarily about power, even though some kind of authority is always required for teaching and guiding others effectively, and human weakness is always susceptible to using authority to pursue power. For Catholic theology, papal primacy is a providentially established force within the much more complicated structure of the leadership of all the churches, aimed at keeping the rest of that structure in touch with the apostolic witness, the Scriptures in their original meaning, and the tradition that gives the Scriptures their continuity and relevance through the centuries. Pope John Paul's recent, radically simple redefini-

---

70. See Dom Lanne's response to the article of Horn in *Il Primato del Successore di Pietro*, pp. 213-221. Both Leo and Gregory the Great insisted that one of the main duties of their vicars in distant provinces was to make sure that the bishops there met in synod with the prescribed regularity: see, e.g., Leo, Epp. 6.5; 13.2; 16.7 (synods in Italy); Gregory, Reg. 1.1; 2.41; 4.9; 7.19.

tion of papal primacy in terms of promoting communion, at the end of *Ut Unum Sint,* could really be a description of Leo's desperate labors to facilitate and defend the consensus of the bishops at Chalcedon, or of Gregory's concern to maintain Christian faith and order in places as far apart as Sicily and Britain, in his role as *servus servorum Dei*:

> The mission of the Bishop of Rome within the College of all the Pastors consists precisely in "keeping watch" (*episkopein*) like a sentinel, so that through the efforts of the Pastors, the true voice of Christ the Shepherd may be heard in all the particular Churches. In this way, in each of the particular Churches entrusted to those Pastors, the *una, sancta, catholica et apostolica Ecclesia* is made present. All the Churches are in full and visible communion, because all the Pastors are in communion with Peter and therefore united in Christ.
>
> With the power and the authority without which such an office would be illusory, the Bishop of Rome must ensure the communion of all the Churches. For this reason, he is the first servant of unity. This primacy is exercised on various levels, including vigilance over the handing down of the Word, the celebration of the Liturgy and the Sacraments, the Church's mission, discipline and the Christian life. It is the responsibility of the Successor of Peter to recall the requirements of the common good of the Church, should anyone be tempted to overlook it in the pursuit of personal interests. He has the duty to admonish, to caution and to declare at times that this or that opinion being circulated is irreconcilable with the unity of faith. . . . All this, however, must always be done in communion.[71]

To be the promoter of a genuinely ecumenical, catholic Christian unity today, the papacy and the whole Roman Catholic Church must clearly accept, in a more serious way than it sometimes has up to now, the reality of Christian diversity as something willed by God and compatible with communion. I do not mean that we must simply acquiesce in the growing multiplicity of Christian denominations and sects, or accept denominational or ideological differences as something final. Religious competition, mutual exclusion, and mutual recrimination among Christians can never be taken as normal, and must always challenge us to move toward real reconciliation. In ecumenical relations, however, Catholics will need to find a

---

71. *Ut Unum Sint,* No. 94.

way to understand communion in faith and worship in a way that will not simply eliminate the structures of community life or the liturgical and theological traditions that have been developed in the whole range of "other" Christian churches through the centuries, and to see the Petrine ministry as called to support and enhance these traditions as far as is possible within the boundaries of apostolic faith, rather than to control them. This means a decided change in some deeply ingrained Catholic attitudes, and it means that all Christians will have to learn to discern more clearly what is essential to the tradition of apostolic faith and life from what is simply legitimate and enriching.

To exercise a genuinely Petrine ministry as promoter of communion among all the churches, it will be important for the pope and the whole Catholic community to distinguish more clearly, as the early Christians seem to have done, between different "spheres of activity" in the pope's work. It will be necessary for the pope to draw clear lines between what he does as bishop of Rome and primate of Italy, what he does as head of the Roman Catholic communion or as "patriarch of the West,"[72] and what he does on the most universal level, as promoter of the communion of all Christendom in the faith and life of the apostles. Like the popes of the Patristic period, he will have to develop procedures and conventions suited to the differing needs, styles, and memories of all three of these sectors within the worldwide community of churches in communion with him.

Likewise, it will be imperative for the popes and the whole Roman curial apparatus to develop a genuinely collegial structure of decision making and administration, and a genuinely collegial style of dealing with individual bishops and national bishops' conferences within the Roman Catholic Church, if Pope John Paul's renewed vision of a universal Petrine ministry is to have real credibility. The recent joint statement of the Anglican–Roman Catholic International Commission, "The Gift of Authority," makes the arresting point that "the exercise of ministerial authority within the church, not least by those entrusted with the ministry of *episkope,* has a radically missionary dimension. Authority is exercised within the church for the sake of those outside it, that the gospel may be proclaimed 'in power and in the Holy Spirit and with full conviction' (I Thes 1.5)." (32)

---

72. See Yves Congar, "Le Pape comme patriarche d'Occident: Approche d'une réalité trop négligé," *Istina* 28 (1983): 374-390; Adriano Garuti, *Il Papa Patriarca d'Occidente? Studio storico dottrinale* (Bologna: Edizioni Francescane, 1990).

The Catholic Church needs to hear this and take it seriously; only if our own practice of collegiality and our own respect for both the unity and the diversity of Christian communion at all levels in our own church is publicly recognizable will we be able to enter into a real communion with those who distrust us.

In an age of increasing electronic unity among all cultures and nations, the late twentieth-century public role of the papacy as a symbol of the gospel tradition, as preacher to the world, will undoubtedly remain an indispensable part of the office. Probably few future popes will share the dazzling abilities of the present Holy Father to communicate with crowds, to speak in other languages, to make an impression on the young. But it will doubtless no longer be an option for the bishop of Rome *not* to be a public figure, however much this may trouble some Christians. Precisely in his role as a communicator and preserver of universal Christian values, of the faith and moral convictions shared by *all* who follow Christ, rather than simply of the traditions of a single strand within the Christian tapestry, the pope will fulfill an indispensable role for all the churches. As popes continue to do this, they will have to learn how to include other Christian leaders more fully within that mission, and to do it in a way that reflects Paul's own "mission statement": "We preach not ourselves, but Jesus Christ as Lord, and ourselves as your servants, for Jesus' sake."[73]

The difficulty, of course, is that the ideal of such a ministry of promoting communion seems to lie far beyond the power and the will of any of us, either as Christian individuals or as Christian communities. Disunity, political self-promotion, institutionalism, and denominationalism are part of the sinful fabric of every Christian communion, preventing us from genuinely being what we profess to be. Having fallen into disunion, each of our churches now has a vested interest in maintaining our differences, and probably very few of us have the generosity of heart really to desire the costly transformation and sacrifice of self that the restoration of communion among our churches will require. Yet Christian growth, we know, always begins in the acceptance of some form of death, and Christian unity, under the leadership of one who serves as Peter was called to do, will require constant dying to our pasts and our ambitions on the part of the pope and his curia as well as on the part of all the churches. "Another will gird you," Jesus reminded Peter, "and lead you where you do not wish

---

73. 2 Corinthians 4:5.

to go."[74] Christian faith alone assures us that such a sharing in death is, for us as it was for Peter and Paul, the way to God.

In another remarkable passage near the end of *Ut Unum Sint*, Pope John Paul sets this paradoxical character of a Petrine ministry — a ministry that originates in weakness and is perfected in corporate, interior dying — within the wide context of God's saving plan for the world:

> As heir to the mission of Peter in the Church, which has been made fruitful by the blood of the Princes of the Apostles, the Bishop of Rome exercises a ministry originating in the manifold mercy of God. This mercy converts hearts and pours forth the power of grace where the disciple experiences the bitter taste of his personal weakness and helplessness. The authority proper to this ministry is completely at the service of God's merciful plan, and it must always be seen in this perspective. . . . Associating himself with Peter's threefold profession of love, which corresponds to the earlier threefold denial, his Successor knows that he must be a sign of mercy. His is a ministry of mercy, born of an act of Christ's own mercy.[75]

As we enter a new millennium, urgently in need of communion on all levels of our human existence, let us all indeed ask for God's mercy. Let us pray that both the bishops of Rome and the Christians with whom they are in dialogue may find new energy and new gifts of imagination to find this divine mercy welling up for all of us in this ancient office, and to share it with the world.

74. John 21:18. It is interesting to note that Pope John Paul frequently stresses the centrality of martyrdom in its traditional sense — of suffering and even death for one's faith — to Christian witness. A recent document from the Congregation of the Doctrine of the Faith on the Petrine office speaks, along similar lines, of "the martyrological nature of the priacy" ("Reflections on the Primacy of the Successor of Peter in the Mystery of the Church," sec. 7, appended to *Il Primato del Successore di Pietro*, 498). Perhaps one aspect of this *martyria* will have to be a greater willingness than in the past on the part of the papal bureaucracy to relinquish some of its centralized power in the interest of promoting communion, through greater subsidiarity and collegiality, within the Catholic Church itself.

75. *Ut Unum Sint*, No. 92-93.

The Papacy and Power:
An Anglican Perspective

STEPHEN W. SYKES

In the beautiful expression of Pope Saint Gregory the Great, my ministry is that of *servus servorum Dei*. This designation is the best possible safeguard against the risk of separating power (and in particular the primacy) from ministry. (*Ut Unum Sint*, No. 88)

[Secundum Gregorii Magni Summi Pontificis expolitum effatum ministerium Nostrum significa illud *servus servorum Dei*. Definitio haec optima quidem ratione a periculo eripit ne potestas (primatus potissimum) a ministerio seiungatur. . . .]

This mercy [sc. the manifold mercy of God] converts hearts and pours forth the power of grace where the disciple experiences the bitter taste of his personal weakness and helplessness. The authority proper to this ministry [sc. of the Bishop of Rome] is completely at the service of God's merciful plan and it must always be seen in this perspective. Its power is explained from this perspective. (*Ut Unum Sint*, No. 92)

[In Ecclesia sanguine coryphaeorum Apostolorum alta, Petri muneris heres, Episcopus Romanus ministerium sustinet quod suam ex multiformi Dei misericordia originem ducit, quae corda convertit gratiaeque dat robur ubi quidem discipulus experitur

59

amarum gustatum imbecillitatis suae suaeque miseriae. Huius ministerii auctoritas tota ad serviendum destinatur misericordi Dei consilio atque hoc sensu usque est intellegenda. Per ipsam eius potestas declaratur.]

With the power and the authority without which such an office would be illusory, the Bishop of Rome must ensure the communion of *all* the Churches. (*Ut Unum Sint*, No. 94)

[Potestate et auctoritate, quibus ademptis munus hoc vacuefit, Episcopus Romanus communionem omnium Ecclesiarum praestare debet.]

It has frequently been noted that the encyclical of Pope John Paul II, *Ut Unum Sint*, bears a twofold message. On the one hand, no major papal claim is missing from it; on the other, all traditional papal claims are set in a new context, provided by a strong and prior affirmation of the "power of grace" (84), and accompanied by remarkable acknowledgments of openness to dialogue on the papal office.

Anglicans have given a striking public welcome to the encyclical. In June 1997 the House of Bishops of the Church of England published its response, *May They All Be One*, speaking appreciatively of many of the features of the encyclical, and noting certain areas requiring further study. In August 1998, the Lambeth Conference responded positively to this initiative as well.

In the paper that follows I shall be concerned with one subject mentioned in the encyclical: power (or more accurately, powers) in relation to the papacy. As we have seen, the encyclical acknowledges that there is a risk that power may be separated from ministry. It insists that the authority and power that is proper to the ministry of the bishop of Rome should be seen from the perspective of the power of grace, and in the light of the servant character of the papal office. At the same time, the pope requires real power and authority to exercise his office. That, in brief, is the message of the encyclical that I propose to examine.

The reason for raising this issue is not to be critical of the mere fact that the pope exercises power — the archbishop of Canterbury exercises power, as does the bishop of Ely. Anglicans have their own experience of primatial power and of episcopal power, and it is not my view that the exercise of power by primates or bishops is either in principle theologically objectionable or necessarily despotic in practice. Nor do I discuss this matter with the concealed or overt intention of commending Anglican practice or structures as they exist at the moment. There is evidence that Anglicans are becoming cautiously self-critical about their inability to make binding decisions at a world level. A report of the Inter-Anglican Theological and Doctrinal Commission (the Virginia Report, 1998) spoke of an increasing awareness that issues have arisen, notably in matters of faith, the sacraments, the ordering of ministry, fundamental changes in relationships with other world communions, and ethical matters, that have implications for the unity and interdependence of the Anglican Communion.[1] And it notes that

> in some cases it may be possible and necessary for the universal Church to say with firmness that a particular local practice or theory is incompatible with Christian faith.[2]

Moreover, a 1998 Lambeth Conference resolution very cautiously suggests an enquiry into whether there might be exceptional circumstances in which the archbishop of Canterbury ought to

> exercise an extraordinary ministry of episcopé (pastoral oversight), support and reconciliation with regard to the internal affairs of a Province other than his own for the sake of maintaining communion within the said Province and between the said Province and the rest of the Anglican Communion.[3]

Even if this is hardly the "universal, ordinary and immediate jurisdiction"[4]

---

1. Inter-Anglican Theological and Doctrinal Commission, *The Virginia Report* (Harrisburg, Penn.: Morehouse, 1999), p. 32.

2. The Virginia Report, p. 34.

3. Resolution IV.13, *Called to be One*, p. 31.

4. *Pastor Aeternus*, 3060. "Docemus proinde et declaramus, Ecclesiam Romanam, disponente Domino, super omnes alias ordinariae potestatis obtinere principatum, et hanc Romani Pontificis iurisdictionis potestatem, quae vere episcopalis est, immediatam esse." See also paragraph 3064 of the encyclical. Denzinger-Schönmetzer, *Enchiridion Symbolorum Definitionum et Declarationum de Rebus Fidei et Morum,* editio XXXIV (Herder, 1967), pp. 598-99. Translations may be found in J. Neuner and J. Dupuis, eds., *The Christian Faith in the Doctrinal Documents of the Catholic Church,* rev. ed. (Sydney: Collins, 1983), pp. 230-31.

attributed to the bishop of Rome by the First Vatican Council, it is at least a proposal recognizing that in some circumstances the jurisdiction of a primatial "ordinary" might be appropriate and useful in the Christian church.

Nor would such a ministry be foreign to Anglicanism, at least within a given province. Within the province of Canterbury, for example, Church of England Canon Law gives the archbishop certain metropolitical powers and jurisdiction as "ordinary" during the time of visitation. That is to say, the archbishop of Canterbury has the power, as metropolitan of the archdiocese, to intervene in the affairs of a diocese within his province. It is correct to argue, as Dr. Colin Podmore has recently contended, that "Anglicans who oppose the attachment of jurisdiction to universal primacy have to show why jurisdiction, and in some cases even ordinary jurisdiction, are appropriate at the provincial level, but not at the universal level."[5] So Anglicans cannot have any objection in principle to the mere fact that as universal primate, the bishop of Rome must have certain jurisdictional powers. This is already articulated in ARCIC I, *Authority in the Church II* 1981, paragraph 20. There are moral limits to its exercise; Anglicans are entitled to an assurance that "theological, liturgical and other traditions which they value" would not be suppressed (paragraph 22). The essential point remains, however, that jurisdiction is only possible by virtue of jurisdictional powers. The first intention of this essay is to make the point that these powers are an unavoidable, but frequently avoided, concomitant of the debate about the papacy.

In the first section I shall argue that the main tradition of the churches is to speak directly and realistically of power or powers in the church. Second, I will explore the avoidance of this topic in ARCIC documents. In the last section I will outline the tasks that remain.

According to the 1566 Catechism of the Council of Trent, "A visible church requires a visible head: therefore the Saviour appointed Peter head and pastor of all the faithful, when he committed to his care the feeding of all the sheep, in such ample terms that he willed the very same power of ruling and governing the entire Church to descend to Peter's successors."[6]

---

5. Colin Podmore, ed., *Community, Unity, Communion: Essays in Honour of Mary Tanner* (London: Church House Publishing, 1998), p. 290.

6. *The Catechism of the Council of Trent* (Rockford, Ill.: Tan Books & Publishers, 1982), p. 104.

Compare with this passage the words of Article XXVIII of the Augsburg Confession (Ecclesiastical Power), citing the English translation of the Latin version:

> Our teachers assert that according to the Gospel the power of the keys or the power of bishops is a power or command of God to preach the Gospel, to forgive and retain sins, and to administer and distribute the sacraments.[7]

> [Sic autem sentiunt, potestatem clavium seu potestatem episcoporum iuxta evangelium potestatem esse seu mandatum Dei praedicandi evangelii, remittendi et retinendi peccata, et administrandi sacramenta.][8]

What is notable about both those quotations is their unabashed use of the Latin *potestas* and (in the German text of the Augsburg Confession) the German *Macht*. It is a commonplace of contemporary theology that these are difficult, indeed embarrassing words. Recently Michael Buckley has recognized the centrality of the issue of power *(potestas)*, and the relative dearth of treatments of the subject in Catholic theology.[9] He is also explicit about the acute difficulty of treating the subject in anything other than "a defensive, aggressive, minatory, or self-serving way."[10] At the same time, his treatment of papal primacy, though profound in many other ways, leaves the precise question of power almost untouched. This issue is addressed more directly by Klaus Schatz, who suggests that we might ask

> [w]hether the charism of the Roman Church does not consist at least in part in its refusal to suppress or ignore the problems of institutionalization and power as if they were foreign to the gospel — especially since the problem of power continually arises in the Church, whether in the form of dominance over the Church exercised by the Christian emperors or in the established Churches of the Reformation. The con-

7. John H. Leith, ed., *Creeds of the Churches: A Reader in Christian Doctrine from the Bible to the Present*, 3rd ed. (Atlanta: John Knox Press, 1982), p. 98.

8. The Diet of Augsburg, 1530, in B. J. Kidd, ed., *Documents Illustrative of the Continental Reformation* (Oxford: Clarendon Press, 1911; repr. 1967), §VII, paragraph 3.

9. Michael J. Buckley SJ, *Papal Primacy and the Episcopate: Towards a Relational Understanding* (New York: Crossroad, 1998), p. 23.

10. *Papal Primacy and the Episcopate*, p. 23.

crete legal and institutional shape of primacy with all its claims to power, may well be the precondition and the price to be paid, in a real Church of sinners and even "sinful structures," so that the universal Church may remain a concrete and not an abstract reality, one that cannot be absorbed into the state or national order but instead preserves its own independence.[11]

How the "power of ruling and governing" has been, or ought to be, exercised within the church is a central issue. But the first observation to be made must concern the serious gulf that separates the modern use of the word "power" from its use in earlier centuries. The point can be made by reference to a sequence of texts. The first is St. Matthew 28:18, "All power (εξουσια) is given to me in heaven and on earth." This term was translated into the Latin *"potestas,"* which together with "virtus," was the usual rendering of either the Greek δυναμισ or εξουσια. The second text is from Pope Innocent III (1198-1216): "Others are called to the role of caring, but only Peter is raised to the fullness of power. Now therefore you see who is the servant who is set over the household, truly the Vicar of Jesus, the successor of Peter, the Christ of the Lord, the God of Pharaoh."[12] As Klaus Schatz has written in commentary on this innovatory title, "Its exclusive nature leads to the very dangerous elevation that threatens to place the papal office above the Church rather than in the Church."[13]

The third text, which has already been cited above, is from *Ut Unum Sint.* Here the pope asserts that the manifold mercy of God "converts hearts and pours forth the power of grace where the disciple experiences the bitter taste of his personal weakness and helplessness." The authority of the ministry of the bishop of Rome, who is heir to the mission of Peter in the church, "is completely at the service of God's merciful plan and it must always be seen in this perspective. Its power is explained from this perspective" (92). The pope heightens confusion when he uses the same word "power" without further explanation in reference to the risen Christ, to the claimed plentitude of power of the medieval pope, and to the grace of God

11. K. Schatz, *Papal Primacy From its Origins to the Present,* tr. J. A. Otto and L. M. Maloney (Collegeville, Minn.: Liturgical Press, 1996). p. 38.

12. Quoted in C. Morris, *The Papal Monarchy: the Western Church from 1050 to 1250* (Oxford: Clarendon Press, 1991), p. 43.

13. Schatz, *Papal Primacy From its Origins to the Present,* p. 93.

in relation to the power of the servant ministry of the modern pope. The theological meaning of power does not persist in a cultural vacuum across twenty centuries; most modern readers of texts do not read the word "power" without thoughts of Machiavelli, Hobbes, Nietzsche, Weber, and Foucault.

Nevertheless, the language of power, carrying an extraordinary range of ideological connotations, is the language of the third chapter of the constitution *Pastor Aeternus,* of the first Vatican Council, approved on July 18, 1870, on the power and nature of the primacy (De vi et ratione primatus Romani Pontificis):

> If anyone says that the Roman Pontiff has only the office of inspection and direction, but not the full and supreme power of jurisdiction over the whole Church, not only in matters that pertain to faith and morals, but also in matters that pertain to the discipline and government of the Church throughout the whole world; or if anyone say that he has only a more important part and not the complete fullness of this supreme power; or if anyone says that this power is not ordinary and immediate either over each and every Church or over each and every shepherd and faithful, *anathema sit.*[14]

In an exceptionally fruitful work, *The Bishop of Rome* (1982), Père Jean Tillard has insisted that this celebrated paragraph concerning the "pontifical powers" be contextualized by earlier paragraphs insisting on the vocation of the church of Rome to guard the unity of the church by fidelity to the apostolic faith. Both the bishop of Rome and the local diocesan bishop have ordinary and immediate powers. Tillard argues that a careful analysis of the debates at Vatican I shows that pontifical powers only exist to make it possible to carry out the papal office (*officium, munus*), which is that of enabling each local bishop to build up his diocese into the *koinonia* of the churches.[15] Similarly, Professor Hermann Pottmeyer has recently argued that it was not the intention of the council to assert the absolute sovereignty and monarchy of the pope; that it accommodated a plurality of possible forms of papacy; and that Vatican

---

14. Neuner and Dupuis, *The Christian Faith,* paragraph 830, p. 231 (corresponds to paragraph 3064 of the Latin text in Denzinger-Schönmetzer).

15. Jean Tillard, *The Bishop of Rome,* trans. John de Satgé (London: SPCK, 1983), p. 148.

centralization was not the direct consequence of the theology of the papacy.[16]

There is something of a procedural difficulty here, relating to the precise interpretation of texts that are not part of Anglican history. It is plain that the texts are of exceptional authority in the Roman Catholic Church. To a large extent — perhaps to too large an extent — they implicitly determine the agenda of such bodies as ARCIC, even to the exclusion of more modest but nonetheless real traditions of Anglicanism. Anglicans view with appreciation, but also a certain detachment, the huge amount of detailed scholarly effort expended to elucidate the claims of Vatican I. It is not always clear to them whether the endorsement of an ARCIC text containing an interpretation of Vatican I implies the acceptance of the authoritative status of the *text* of Vatican I.

But Anglican history underwent a momentous development of its own in the later nineteenth century. It is noteworthy that, at the same time that Pope Pius IX was considering the summoning of a council of bishops, it was becoming obvious that there was a need for an international gathering of Anglican bishops. The first Lambeth Conference was called for 1867. As Owen Chadwick has written: "Here then is already an Anglican worldwide church which needs a government."[17] But this could not be a government with great claims of authority for itself; the archbishop of Canterbury who called the meeting said that it was for "brotherly counsel and encouragement." Three conferences later in 1897, a growing experience of the consequences of the conference, which from the first had considered disciplinary matters of importance to all the member churches, led to the following resolution:

> That, recognising the advantages which have accrued to the Church from the meetings of the Lambeth Conferences, we are of opinion that it is of great importance to the well-being of the Church that there should be from time to time meetings of the bishops of the whole Anglican Communion for the consideration of questions that may arise affecting the Church of Christ (Resolution 1).[18]

16. Hermann J. Pottmeyer, *Towards a Papacy in Communion* (New York: Crossroad, 1998), pp. 70-75.

17. "Introduction," in R. Coleman, ed., *Resolutions of the Twelve Lambeth Conferences 1867-1988* (Toronto: Anglican Book Centre, 1992), p. v.

18. Coleman, *Resolutions of the Twelve Lambeth Conferences 1867-1988*, p. 16.

A meeting which began by claiming that it had no authority acquired an authority of competence. In Owen Chadwick's words, "some of the most important parts of authority are not based on the law."[19] Thus began a process of convergence between traditional claims of the papacy and the newer Anglican exploration of the possibility of an international authority.

I turn now to examine the issue of the power of the papacy as it has been discussed in ARCIC statements, notably in *The Final Report* of ARCIC I and in the recently published *Gift of Authority: Authority in the Church III,* of ARCIC II.[20] One feature is immediately obvious: the word "power" has virtually disappeared behind the preferred term "authority." The only explicit reference to the long tradition of defining primacy in relation to power *(potestas)* appears in the definition of jurisdiction, "the authority or power *(potestas)* necessary for the effective fulfilment of an office" *(Authority in the Church I,* Elucidation, 6).[21] The second statement on authority in the church reaffirms the alternative, "authority or power," as though the concepts were identical in meaning. Here it becomes quite explicit that the preferred term is "authority," and moreover that "power" is used in such negatively charged phrases as "arbitrary power of one man over the freedom of others" (17) and "autocratic power over the Church" (19).

The most recent ARCIC statement on authority, *The Gift of Authority: Authority in the Church III,* continues this negative usage. "The jurisdiction of bishops," it reads, "is one consequence of the call they have received to lead their churches in an authentic 'Amen'; it is not arbitrary power given to one person over the freedom of others."[22] It is notable too that the only positive connotation given to "power" is in the phrases "the Risen Christ empowered [the disciples] to spread the gospel," "the power of the Spirit," and (citing 1 Thess. 1:5), "in power and the Holy Spirit" (paragraph 32).

Why the use of the word "authority" when the tradition on which the statements purport to comment explicitly use the word "power"? The reason lies substantially in the modern connotations of "power," which, as

19. Coleman, *Resolutions of the Twelve Lambeth Conferences 1867-1988,* p. x.

20. Second Anglican–Roman Catholic International Commission, *The Gift of Authority: Authority in the Church III* (London: CTS; Toronto: Anglican Book Centre; New York: Church Publishing Inc., 1999).

21. Anglican–Roman Catholic International Commission, *The Final Report* (London: CTS/SPCK, 1982), p. 74.

22. *The Gift of Authority,* paragraph 36, p. 27.

Raymond Aron has observed, have become negative and threatening.[23] It is for this reason that the documents naturally associate "power" with "arbitrary" and "autocratic" — except when citing scriptural verses about the power of God. Perhaps this is why the Australian priest and historian Paul Collins, when writing a highly critical book about what the papacy has become, gave it the title *Papal Power.* [24]

The unsatisfactoriness of this procedure manifests itself in that exactly the same difficulty of arbitrariness and autocracy now attaches to the doctrine of God. Jürgen Moltmann discusses this problem explicitly in several of his works, not hesitating to relate the negative aspects of divine monarchy to monarchial church government.[25] The ARCIC documents ignore this even more fundamental theological problem, simply assuming that one may speak of the power of God, of the Spirit, and of divine "empowerment" without any suspicion that the linking of divine power to the jurisdictional powers of any bishop or of the bishop of Rome might give rise to objections. It is ARCIC's position that authority in the church is divine authority: "The root of all true authority is thus the activity of the triune God, who authors life in all its fullness."[26] In the first statement on authority it affirms that

> the Spirit of the risen Lord, who indwells the Christian community, continues to maintain the people of God in obedience to the Father's will. He safeguards their faithfulness to the revelation of Jesus Christ and equips them for their mission in the world. By this action of the Holy Spirit the authority of the Lord is active in the Church.[27]

In the third statement, by means of an exegesis of 2 Corinthians 1:18-20, it is argued that the believers' response of "Amen" to the action of God is a sharing in Christ's own "Amen," and thus carries Christ's own authority.

> The Spirit of Christ endows each bishop with the pastoral authority needed for the effective exercise of *episcopē* within a local church. . . . De-

23. R. Aron, quoted in S. Lukes, *Power: A Radical View* (Basingstoke: Macmillan Education, 1974; repr. 1988), p. 253.

24. Paul Collins, *Papal Power: A Proposal for Change in Catholicism's Third Millennium* (London: Fount, 1997).

25. See J. Moltmann on the criticism of clerical monotheism in *The Trinity and the Kingdom of God* (London: SCM Press, 1981), pp. 191-222.

26. *The Gift of Authority,* paragraph 7, p. 13.

27. *Authority in the Church I,* in *The Final Report,* p. 53.

cisions taken by the bishop in performing this task have an authority which the faithful have a duty to receive and accept.[28]

At this point there is an obvious but unacknowledged entangling of "authority" with what can be perceived sociologically as power. To legitimate the decisions of a bishop by identifying their source in the Spirit of Christ, and then to require the duty that they be received and accepted by the faithful, is to invest the bishop with remarkable power. Not to speak of it as power, to deny that it is arbitrary or autocratic (though it plainly could be), and to assert that it is only exercised as service, is to engage in a dangerous form of disguise. Had the commission faced the issue of power straightforwardly, it would have had to confront the notion explored in modern Anglo-American sociology that those attempting to defend and advance their own power often emphasize its service component.[29] It would also have had to consider the whole issue of the various ways in which the powerful strive to conceal the reality of their power from those over whom they exercise it.[30]

The advantages of continuing to use the word "power" are twofold. First of all, it obliges one to deal explicitly with the theological and ideological tradition by which the "plenitude of power" came to be attributed to the pope. Secondly, one is also forced to consider carefully the way in which the church progressively lost the struggle to define the word "power" in its own manner, and has consequently entered into a state of deep ambivalence about the distribution and exercise of power in the church.

Finally, we must examine the tasks that still remain along the pathway to more complete convergence of the churches. In the first place, it will be necessary to reconceptualize the treatment of "authority" and "leadership" in the church in terms of a biblical and postmodern understanding of the ambivalence and plurality of created powers. In the Canaanite understanding, there was a variety of deities that met in council. Besides Baal, Mot, Yanim and El, there were the sons of gods, the hosts of heaven. The members of the council interacted and competed, while El presided. The New Testament retains this pluralism in its references to

28. *Authority in the Church II*, 17, in *The Final Report*, p. 89.
29. Lukes, *Power*, p. 7.
30. On the issue of concealment of power, see the works of French sociologist Maurice Duverger.

"principalities and powers." Though the background to this expression is obscure, it seems clear that the created order contains a variety of powers. These are not the malign, independent beings of a dualistic worldview, but may be brought within the scope of God's reign — hence the divine origin of "the powers that be" (Rom. 13). But there is an ambivalence about the powers that is only resolved eschatologically; Christ is destined to reign "until God has put all enemies under his feet" (1 Cor. 15:25).

The ambivalence and pluralism of the powers in biblical thought correspond closely to the modern distinction between modern and post-modern views of power. In the sovereignty conception, power is unified and polarized, as in the thought of Hobbes. It lends itself to zero-sum calculation, so if one party has more of it, then another party must have less. Power is also necessarily domination. Theologically, this trend in Western thought has proved to be extremely problematic. It explains, of course, the malign and negative connotations of the word "power" and its ready association (which we have noted even in the ARCIC documents) with auto-cratic and arbitrary behavior. To escape from this, some theologians have gone so far as to claim that "powerlessness" is the only possible stance of the Christian. This is both inherently implausible, and contradicts clear strands of biblical teaching. As we have already remarked, it creates a virtu-ally unbridgeable gulf between the traditional discussion of *potestas* and modern treatment of the question, a gulf which is not adequately covered by the deployment of the term "authority."

Postmodern thinking, following remarkably in the steps of Machiavelli, has by contrast emphasized that all human beings exist in a network of plural powers, some of which exercise considerable influence over human beings, but virtually all of which can be resisted by counter-vailing forces. This is both a more credible account of the situation, and has the substantial merit of reconnecting the discussion with the biblical tradition. Some powers are malign and to be strenuously resisted; others are benign and can properly be appropriated or reinforced. Human beings have powers at their disposal, though many of these powers are ambiva-lent, and need vigilant and disciplined attention. But all human beings are set within conflicts both in the external and internal fora, and these con-flicts are only to be resolved at the eschaton.

Secondly, the doctrine of the church must be explicitly rooted in the doctrine of creation, as well as the doctrines of redemption and sanctifica-tion. The reason for this is that only a doctrine of creation will alert the theologian to the plurality and ambivalence of the powers exercised within the church, as in any human organization. It is, of course, a matter of ordinary observation that powers are distributed and exercised by a variety of agents within large organizations. They are the stuff of gossip and jokes; but sociologically acute enquirers take note of them as well. For example, Jesuit political scientist Thomas J. Reese details (in an undoubtedly biased fashion) the normal workings of a large centralized bureaucracy in his book *Inside the Vatican.*[31] But what is unmistakable is that the powers of the papacy confer powers of various kinds upon the bureaucracy. No sociologically informed observer of a large organization would imagine otherwise. But the mystery and tragedy is that this fact has so far escaped theological interpretation.

This situation can only be addressed when some of the deficiencies of a *communio* understanding of the church are recognized. Scholars have long realized that the *koinonia* model is christologically and pneumatologically oriented. What is missing from it is, in fact, the perspective of creation: that the powers that are exercised in the church in virtue of the victory of Christ and the empowering of the Holy Spirit are still ambivalent so long as the church is *in via*. We need to build an explicitly theological connection between the known fact that some of the power exercised in the bureaucracy is misused or at least ambivalent, and the high-flown christological language of service or of grace. Not to do so is to fall into the trap of concealment, and to encourage the response of suspicion and cynicism. The powers available within the church need a more honest account and a more realistic theological appraisal. Only the doctrine of creation can provide this in its application to the life of the church.

Thirdly, the bureaucracy implied in papal powers must be revisited with the aid of sociological tools. Only such an open acknowledgment will end the offering of a frustrating and in the end simplistic choice between obedience to authority or autonomous individualism. This emerges from time to time even within *The Gift of Authority,* which is at some pains to emphasize the mutuality characterizing the life of the church:

> The Holy Spirit works through all members of the community, using the gifts he gives to each for the good of all. In each community there is an

31. Thomas Reese SJ, *Inside the Vatican: The Politics and Organization of the Catholic Church* (Cambridge, Mass.: Harvard University Press, 1996).

exchange, a mutual give-and-take, in which bishops, clergy and lay people receive from as well as give to others within the whole body (28).

Mutuality is closely related to the *sensus fidelium,* and the document is both correct and helpful in insisting that Roman Catholics and Anglicans need to make a deliberate effort to retrieve this teaching (31).

But in other places the report clearly demonstrates the other way of thinking and emphasizes the passivity and docility of the rest of the church in the face of episcopal or primatial responsibility to exercise authority. It becomes unclear whether there is any possibility that the mutuality emphasized in parts of the document might lead to a demurral from, or even challenge to, the "authoritative" teaching of the bishops. One remarkable paragraph states both that the reception of teaching is vital to the process, and that authoritative teaching is to be welcomed by the people of God as the gift of the Holy Spirit (43). A consistent interpretation would suggest that only such teaching as expresses the apostolic faith would be so welcomed, or that bishops would only ever pronounce teaching to be authoritative if the consensus had already judged the matter to be so. In either case, the report ignores the possibility of conflict and disagreement, demonstrating a failure to move beyond the dichotomy between obedience and individualism, docility and suspicion.

In the fourth place, we should consider the importance of what could be called "institutional humility." The way in which institutions elicit and nurture the loyalty of their members is well known. (In English collegiate universities undergraduates who have been allocated to colleges on a random basis come to believe within two weeks that their college is undoubtedly the best in the university.) Men and women who have been born in and nourished by a particular church naturally assume that its doctrines, worship, and structures are the most desirable in Christendom. But the lessons of Lessing's parable of the ring apply to the churches as well as to the religious. The elements of institutional humility are indeed striking in *Ut Unum Sint.*

Similarly in *The Gift of Authority* there is an impressive paragraph acknowledging not only the individual frailty of the ministers of the church but also the presence of human weakness and sin in church structures:

Human weakness and sin not only affect individual ministers: they can distort the human structuring of authority (cf. Matt. 23). Therefore, loyal criticism and reforms are sometimes needed, following the example of Paul (cf. Gal. 2:11-14). The consciousness of human frailty in the exercise of authority ensures that Christian ministers remain open to criticism and renewal and above all to exercising authority according to the example and mind of Christ.[32]

These remarks are both courageous and necessary. But they still focus too closely upon individual frailty, and fall a considerable distance short of the language of Article XIX of the Thirty-nine Articles, which reads:

The visible Church of Christ is a congregation of faithful men, in which the pure Word of God is preached, and the Sacraments be duly ministered according to Christ's ordinance in all those things that of necessity are requisite to the same.

Then it adds:

As the Church of Jerusalem, Alexandria, and Antioch have erred; so also the Church of Rome hath erred, not only in their living and manner of Ceremonies, but also in matters of Faith.

The unstated implication of this polemically phrased article is the possibility that the Church of England, too, is capable of error.[33]

I have already remarked on the fact that in Anglican–Roman Catholic dialogue it seems to have become a norm that Roman Catholic doctrines and documentation govern the agenda. But this is an instance where it is important to consider a long-held Anglican tradition, that of self-criticism. Of course we must not be governed by sixteenth-century controversies and language; nor should we return to judging the adequacy of new treatments of issues by the terminology of the past. This was what was so disappointing about the official Vatican response to ARCIC I.[34] But in the

32. *The Gift of Authority,* paragraph 48, p. 35. Compare to *Authority in the Church I,* paragraph 7, p. 55, in *The Final Report,* p. 8.

33. Oliver O'Donovan, *On the 39 Articles: A Conversation with Tudor Christianity* (Carlisle: Paternoster Press, 1986; repr. 1993). See chapter on "The Disappearance of the Invisible Church (Article 19)," pp. 88-96.

34. Christopher Hill and Edward Yarnold, SJ, eds., *Anglicans and Roman Catholics: The Search for Unity* (London: SPCK/CTS, 1994), pp. 156-166. Henry Chadwick, commenting as a member of ARCIC, had this to say: "What is being said is that the language is not identical with that familiar from the definitions of Trent or Vatican I, and that in conse-

matter of institutional humility we are dealing with a deeply laid Anglican assumption that even solemnly exercised, divinely bestowed acts of jurisdiction are not protected from error, and they may be properly resisted with loyalty.

Finally, I wish to draw attention to the importance of a distinction adopted by Michael Buckley, in his discussion of papal primacy, between "habitual" and "substitutional" functions of jurisdiction. He defines "habitual" use of papal powers as follows:

> to foster the unity of [the bishop's] brothers, not of his children — a unity in their faith and mutual charity — and with his brothers in college the unity of the churches and of the entire Church. . . . Supervising the direction of developed and free human beings and particular churches towards the common good of that *communio* that is of all the churches.[35]

The "substitutional" use of his powers would occur in exceptional circumstances,

> when other structures of leadership and service have broken down and the unity in faith and communion of the episcopate or of the faithful is severely threatened.[36]

The ARCIC documents make very much the same distinction.[37] The Virginia Report makes clear, in the context of an explicit embracing of subsidiarity in its ecclesiological relevance, that there could be occasions when a higher authority had the duty to intervene, and needed the powers to do so, in the life of a more local body under certain exceptional circumstances.

It is this right and duty to which the pope refers in *Ut Unum Sint:* "with the power and authority without which such an office would be illusory, the bishop of Rome must ensure the communion of *all* the Churches"

---

quence some few concepts associated by the Vatican with a generalised Protestantism (and not mentioned directly by ARCIC) have not been expressly excluded. For the Vatican, therefore, ARCIC's account is not so much wrong as less than full" (p. 212).

35. Buckley, *Papal Primacy and the Episcopate*, p. 65.

36. Buckley, *Papal Primacy and the Episcopate*, p. 64.

37. See *Authority in the Church II*, paragraph 20 — "the right in special cases to intervene," in *The Final Report*, p. 90.

(94). It is notable and surely correct that the pope uses the word "power" in this context, and that there is an explicit realism about its use. It is in this passage too that the proper sociological cost has to be paid for connecting the traditional use of the word *potestas* in papal documents with the hard, practical realities of decisive intervention. The plain difficulty in the acceptance of such powers, which the Anglican Communion also tentatively is beginning to admit that it needs, is the insidious way in which "substitutional" powers become "habitual," and having become habitual are extensively and tediously justified forever.

In the years since Vatican I, Anglicans and Roman Catholics have been engaged in a slow process of convergence. Still, a good deal remains to be honestly and seriously confronted in the historical and conceptual problems of power.

Veni Creator Spiritus

Ut Unum Sint in Light of "Faith and Order" — or "Faith and Order" in Light of Ut Unum Sint?

GEOFFREY WAINWRIGHT

At the meeting of the WCC Commission on Faith and Order in Lima, Peru, in January 1982, during one of the last plenary discussions on the nearly completed document *Baptism, Eucharist and Ministry*, Professor J. Robert Wright of the Episcopal Church, USA, asked that a paragraph be inserted on the otherwise unmentioned topic of the Petrine ministry, which Catholics locate in the see of Rome. Baptist and Orthodox members of the commission sprang up to oppose the move. As chairman of the smaller editorial group working on *BEM*, I asked for counsel from the plenary session. The minutes record that "while recognizing the vital importance of the issue of the Petrine ministry and the excellent work done on this issue in various bilateral conversations, the prevailing argument was that the subject had not previously been on the Faith and Order agenda and was of such significance that no hasty attempt should be made to incorporate a reference to the issue in the present document."[1] No doubt the question of Petrine ministry was on Anglican minds because it had been treated — under the principal rubric of primacy — in the 1976 and 1981 statements on "Authority in the Church" that were to be included in *The Final Report* of the first Anglican–Roman Catholic In-

---

1. *Towards Visible Unity: Commission on Faith and Order, Lima 1982*, volume 1: Minutes and Addresses, Faith and Order Paper No. 112, ed. Michael Kinnamon (Geneva: World Council of Churches, 1982), pp. 80-82.

ternational Commission.[2] Certainly, several responses to *BEM* by the provinces of the Anglican Communion expressed regret at the absence of this theme from the Lima document. This was notably the case with (yes) the Episcopal Church, USA, but also the Scottish Episcopal Church, the Church of the Province of New Zealand, and (ever so obliquely) the Church of England.[3] As the Petrine ministry gradually became part of the broader ecumenical conversation, multilaterally as well as in bilateral dialogues to which the Roman Catholic Church was party, reference was often made to the implications at the universal level of the general principle formulated in *BEM* that "the ordained ministry should be exercised in a personal, collegial and communal way."[4]

Since 1968, the Faith and Order Commission has included twelve Roman Catholics as full members, officially appointed, among its complement of 120. As a participant in the *BEM* core group, I can testify to the efficacy of several of them. Their continuing discretion is shown by the fact that the major post-Lima project on the apostolic faith, even in the second version of the study document *Confessing the One Faith* (1991), still made no mention of the Petrine office in its exposition of the ecclesiological clauses of the Nicene-Constantinopolitan Creed.[5] By the time of the Fifth

---

2. *Anglican–Roman Catholic International Commission: The Final Report — Windsor, September 1981* (London: SPCK, and Catholic Truth Society, 1982), pp. 47-100.

3. *Churches Respond to BEM: Official Responses to the "Baptism, Eucharist and Ministry" Text*, volume 2, Faith and Order Paper No. 132, ed. Max Thurian (Geneva: WCC, 1986), pp. 61, 50, and 68, respectively, and volume 3, Faith and Order Paper No. 135, ed. Max Thurian (Geneva: WCC, 1987), p. 77. As a mischievous footnote to a footnote, it may be observed that exactly three of those churches took the lead in developments within Anglicanism that run counter to current Roman Catholic positions: ECUSA was the first to ordain women to the diaconate, to the presbyterate, and to the episcopate; New Zealand elected the first woman diocesan bishop; and at the Lambeth Conference of 1998 the Scottish primus was the most outspoken advocate of homosexual causes. The second Anglican–Roman Catholic International Commission returned briefly to the theme of the universal primacy of the bishop of Rome in its Report *The Gift of Authority* (dated September 1998, published May 1999), paragraphs 45-48, 60-62, notably: "The reception of the primacy of the Bishop of Rome entails the recognition of this specific ministry of the universal primate [to 'discern and declare, with the assured assistance and guidance of the Holy Spirit, in fidelity to Scripture and Tradition, the authentic faith of the whole Church, that is, the faith proclaimed from the beginning']. We believe that this is a gift to be received by all the churches" (paragraph 47).

4. *Baptism, Eucharist and Ministry*, Faith and Order Paper No. 111 (Geneva: WCC, 1982), pp. 25f. ("Ministry," paragraphs 26-27).

5. *Confessing the One Faith: An Ecumenical Explication of the Apostolic Faith as it is*

World Conference on Faith and Order, held at Santiago de Compostela in August 1993, the topic, though still not explicitly so phrased, had crept onto the agenda. Under the keyword of *koinonia,* the report of section one remarked that "the concept of communion can help us overcome traditional dichotomies between the institutional and the charismatic, the local and the universal, conciliarity and primacy, etc. This concept, if it is used creatively in ecclesiology, would also help to overcome any views of ministry, authority and structure in the Church, which hinder progress towards unity."[6] The report of section two, under the heading of "confessing the one faith to God's glory," deals in part with "structures serving unity" and moves on from the local and regional levels to say,

> The connection of personal, collegial, and synodical responsibility concerning teaching and unity of the Church is of fundamental importance also for Church structures on the universal level. Here we recall once more the Ecumenical Councils of the Ancient Church, in which, in principle, representatives of all churches participated. Today, ecumenical dialogues should take up once again the topic of a service to the universal unity of the Church on the basis of the truth of the Gospel. Such service should be carried out in a pastoral way — that is, as "presiding in love." It should also have the function of speaking for Christianity to the world at large, under conditions which need to be more precisely defined. This ministry must be bound to the community of all the churches and their leaders and is in service to the whole people of God.
>
> One can rightly affirm that each local church is a concrete manifestation of the catholic Church, insofar as it is in communion with all the other churches. This affirmation raises the question of the presidency of this communion of churches. Accordingly, to such church structures on the universal level there must correspond the communion of all local churches and church communities. By means of mutual communication, a universal participation in the manifold efforts for the enculturation of the Gospel takes place. Without such living communion, the structure of the universal Church would not be credible.

Confessed in the Nicene-Constantinopolitan Creed (381), Faith and Order Paper No. 153 (Geneva: WCC, 1991).

6. *On the Way to Fuller Koinonia: Official Report of the Fifth World Conference on Faith and Order,* Faith and Order Paper No. 166, ed. Thomas F. Best and Günther Gassmann (Geneva: WCC, 1994), p. 236.

Section two then makes the formal recommendation that "the Faith and Order Commission begin a new study concerning the question of a universal ministry of Christian unity," with the comment that "earlier bilateral and multilateral dialogues, which in general should be more interrelated because of their necessary complementarity, can form a valuable point of departure for this new study."[7]

When, in his 1995 encyclical *Ut Unum Sint,* Pope John Paul II issued his striking invitation to "a patient and fraternal dialogue" on the universal ministry of unity that the Roman see claims and offers, he explicitly invoked the Santiago recommendation.[8] In turn, Mary Tanner, then moderator of Faith and Order, invoked the papal encyclical in advising the WCC's commission in plenary session at Moshi, Tanzania, in 1996 that, given the Catholic Church's position that communion with the church of Rome and the bishop of Rome is an essential requisite of full communion, "it is incumbent on all of us to engage with that challenge, whatever our tradition." Tanner judged that papal "primacy" must be considered "in the context of conciliarity," apparently understood in accordance with the vision of ecclesial unity proposed by the WCC's 1975 Nairobi Assembly as "a conciliar fellowship of local churches which are themselves truly united."[9] The Faith and Order board, at its meetings in 1996 and 1997, discussed the making of a response to *Ut Unum Sint;* and after its 1998 meeting it sent a reply to the Vatican as "an indication of ways in which the encyclical is in harmony with the views of the Faith and Order Commission," welcoming the bishop of Rome's "own and his Church's ongoing commitment to the search for visible unity." Faith and Order was grateful for the recognition that "mutual help" was needed, although it naturally felt obliged to point out that the other "ecclesial communities" believed by the Roman Catholic Church to be in various ways defective believe themselves to be "true churches within the wholeness of the Church of Jesus Christ,

---

7. *On the Way to Fuller Koinonia,* p. 243.

8. *Ut Unum Sint,* No. 89. That this was not John Paul II's first move to put the matter on the ecumenical agenda is recalled by Pierre Duprey, "The Encyclical *Ut Unum Sint* and Faith and Order," in *Community, Unity, Communion: Essays in Honour of Mary Tanner,* ed. Colin Podmore (London: Church House Publishing, 1998), pp. 216-223.

9. Mary Tanner, "Continuity and Newness: From Budapest to Moshi," in *Faith and Order in Moshi: The 1996 Commission Meeting,* Faith and Order Paper No. 177, ed. Alan Falconer (Geneva: WCC, 1998), pp. 29-39.

though hoping to receive gifts from one another in progress to the visible unity of the Church."[10]

Faith and Order then hinted at a substantive treatment of a universal ministry of unity in its broader work in a tentative text issuing in November 1998 from the major post-Santiago project on ecclesiology, *The Nature and Purpose of the Church: A Stage on the Way to a Common Statement.*[11] The prominence of problem over promise, however, is epitomized by the fact that most of the hints are set off in boxes listing "areas where differences remain both within and between churches."[12] Thus in the box labeled "Diversity," Roman claims to "primacy" are listed among the special "emphases" characteristic of different traditions, where the issue is posed in terms of the possibility of the maintenance of such emphases in an enriching rather than a divisive way:

> Diversities in expression of the Gospel, in words and in actions, enrich the common life. Particular emphases today are carried in the life and witness of the different churches: for example, the holiness tradition by the Methodists, the doctrine of justification by faith alone through grace by the Lutherans, the life in the Holy Spirit by the Pentecostals, the ministry of primacy in the service of unity by the Roman Catholic Church, the value of comprehensiveness by the Anglican Communion, the doctrine of deification coupled with that of "synergy" by the Orthodox, etc. How far are the different emphases conflicting positions or an expression of legitimate diversity? Does the weight placed upon the different emphases obscure the fullness of the Gospel message?
>
> What estimate do Christians place on ecclesial and confessional identity? For some the preservation of such identity, at least for the foreseeable future, and even within a life of *koinonia*, is necessary for safeguarding particular truths and rich legitimate diversities that belong to a life of communion. Others understand the goal of visible communion as

10. See *Minutes of the Meeting of the Faith and Order Board, 7-14 January 1996, Bangkok, Thailand,* Faith and Order Paper No. 172 (Geneva: WCC, 1996), p. 55; *Minutes of the Meeting of the Faith and Order Board, 8-15 January 1997, Abbaye de Fontgombault, France,* Faith and Order Paper No. 178 (Geneva: WCC, 1997), pp. 54-57; and *Minutes of the Meeting of the Faith and Order Board, 9-16 January 1998, Istanbul, Turkey,* Faith and Order Paper No. 180 (Geneva: WCC, 1998), pp. 25-27.

11. *The Nature and Purpose of the Church: A Stage on the Way to a Common Statement,* Faith and Order Paper No. 181 (Geneva: WCC, 1998).

12. *The Nature and Purpose of the Church,* p. 7.

beyond particular ecclesial or confessional identity — a communion in which the riches safeguarded by confessional traditions are brought together in the witness and experience of a common faith and life. For others the model of "reconciled diversity" remains a compelling one. Others fear a particular model of "structural merger" in which the diversity carried by different traditions is suppressed by a rigid uniformity. Most, however, agree that an openness is required about the unity to which God calls us, and that as we move by steps under the guidance of the Holy Spirit (cf. Jn 16:13) the portrait of visible unity will become clearer.

It would, of course, be up to the Roman Catholic Church to say whether it could be satisfied with papal primacy being viewed as a quasi-optional "emphasis." There might seem to be an inherent contradiction between the Roman claim and its expendability.[13] The underlying problem resides in the fact that, as the current document states but does not develop, "churches understand their relation to the one, holy, catholic, and apostolic Church in different ways. This has a bearing upon the way they relate to other churches and their perception of the road to visible unity."[14]

The historically and theologically conflictual situation is described in paragraph 93 of the main text of *The Nature and Purpose of the Church* as part of a more general discussion of patterns of "oversight," but the mention of "the ministry of universal primacy" renders the passage of direct interest to the theme of this conference:

> At the Reformation a pluriform pattern came into being as oversight came to be exercised in a variety of ways in the churches of the Reformation. The Reformers sought to return to the apostolicity of the Church which they considered to have been marred. Pursuing this end, they saw themselves faced with the alternative of either staying within the inher-

---

13. For their part, Lutherans also might have an analogous difficulty with the listing of "justification by faith alone through grace" — long viewed as the *"articulus stantis vel cadentis ecclesiae"* — among the adiaphora.

14. *The Nature and Purpose of the Church,* pp. 30f. So far, the Faith and Order study on ecclesiology has not faced up to this underlying problem, despite the hinted awareness of it also in the board's response to *Ut Unum Sint.* For a historical and theological typology of ecclesial self-understandings, and concomitant approaches to unity, see Geoffrey Wainwright, "Church," in *Dictionary of the Ecumenical Movement,* ed. Nicholas Lossky et al. (Geneva: WCC; Grand Rapids: Eerdmans, 1991), pp. 159-167.

ited church structures or remaining faithful to the apostolicity of the
Church, and thus accepted a break with the overall structure of the
Church, including the ministry of universal primacy.[15]

So described, the problem seems to be chiefly a Western one, with regard
to the relation between *episkopē*, episcopacy, and the historic episcopal
succession; but the mention of universal primacy suggests that the conflict about oversight extends also *mutatis mutandis* to the relations between the Roman Catholic Church and the Eastern Orthodox churches.

On the positive side, the Faith and Order text of 1998 records some
apparent, or at least partial, agreements that "the interconnectedness of
the life of the Church is maintained by a ministry of *episkopē*, exercised in
communal, personal, and collegial ways, which sustains a life of interdependence," and that "these dimensions of oversight find expression at the
local, regional, and worldwide levels."[16] Still, the question of "conciliarity
and primacy" is assigned to a problematic "box," where nevertheless a
promising link is suggested by an idea taken up from paragraph 107 of the
main text, namely that "in the local Eucharistic community, conciliarity is
the profound unity in love and truth between the members among themselves and with their presiding minister."[17] The boxed item reads:

> There is still much work to be done to arrive at something like a consen-
> sus between those who do not believe that conciliarity or primacy at a
> world level are necessary and those who believe that full communion
> cannot exist without this link among all the local Eucharistic communi-
> ties. The lack of agreement is not simply between certain families of
> churches but exists within some churches. The way forward involves
> coming to a consensus both within each church and among the
> churches.
>
> Most churches accept that a Eucharist needs a president. Amongst
> these, there are some who go on to say that it follows that a gathering of

15. *The Nature and Purpose of the Church*, p. 46.

16. *The Nature and Purpose of the Church*, p. 48 (paragraphs 96-97). There is a clear
echo here of what *BEM* called the "personal, collegial, and communal" dimensions of "ordained ministry," though the sequence is altered to "communal, personal, and collegial," and
"communal" is given "conciliar or synodal" as synonym(s). The definitions are that "by
synodality (communality) we mean the 'walking together' of all the churches" and "by collegiality, the 'communion' of all those who exercise oversight in them."

17. *The Nature and Purpose of the Church*, p. 53 (paragraph 107).

Eucharistic communities at regional and world levels similarly need a president, in the service of communion. In this perspective, conciliarity implies primacy, and primacy involves conciliarity.[18]

It is not immediately clear just how far the nexus of notions conjoined in the last paragraph cited may underlie a couple of sentences in paragraph 97 of *Ut Unum Sint:* "The Catholic Church, both in her praxis and in her solemn documents, holds that the communion of particular Churches with the Church of Rome, and of their Bishop with the Bishop of Rome, is — in God's plan — an essential requisite of full and visible communion. Indeed full communion, of which the Eucharist is the highest sacramental manifestation, needs to be visibly expressed in a ministry in which all the Bishops recognize that they are united in Christ and all the faithful find confirmation for their faith."

The only other passage in the 1998 Faith and Order document pertaining to our theme is a paragraph about the locus of authority that is contained in a box devoted primarily to the term and reality of the "local church":

Churches differ according to where they perceive authority rests and how decisions are taken. For example, in some traditions authority lies primarily with the local church, in others it is focused in the worldwide college of bishops presided over by a primate, in others it lies in regional autocephalous churches, as well as on a global level through ecumenical councils presided over by a primate. This for some implies a conciliar consensus enlightened by the Holy Spirit as the only criterion of authority. In yet other traditions, authority is dispersed, and the province or a regional unit is the level at which binding decisions are taken.[19]

The foregoing is the sum of what, in 1999, I can report concerning the present state of play in the WCC Commission on Faith and Order in the matter of a universal ministry of unity. Now I will shift perspectives by looking at what Pope John Paul II writes in *Ut Unum Sint* in recognition of the achievements of Faith and Order and in possible stimulus to its further work, with an eye directly or indirectly to the Petrine ministry claimed and

18. *The Nature and Purpose of the Church,* p. 55. Hovering in the background here, of course, is the "eucharistic ecclesiology" developed by Afanasiev, Zizioulas, Tillard, and others.
19. *The Nature and Purpose of the Church,* p. 33.

offered by the Roman see. I will pick out the following ten themes and treat them in the sequence in which they receive principal attention in the pope's ecumenical encyclical of Ascension Day 1995: doctrine; prayer; baptism; Eucharist and the liturgy more generally; visible unity; the relation between Scripture, tradition, and magisterium; the Virgin Mary; saints and martyrs; the Petrine office itself; and the connection between unity and evangelization.

Doctrine

In paragraph 17 of *Ut Unum Sint,* in mentioning "the principal documents of the Commission on Faith and Order and the statements of numerous bilateral dialogues" as a demonstration of "the remarkable progress already made" and "a source of hope inasmuch as they represent a sure foundation for further study," the pope singles out *Baptism, Eucharist and Ministry* (1982) and *Confessing the One Faith* (1991). That recognition immediately precedes the encyclical's section on "the fundamental importance of doctrine" to ecumenism, since "the unity willed by God can be attained only by the adherence of all to the content of revealed faith in its entirety," even while "the content of faith . . . must be translated into all cultures" and its expression renewed "for the sake of transmitting to the people of today the Gospel message in its unchanging meaning" (paragraph 19). We should bear in mind that in the case of *BEM,* the Roman Catholic Church took the unprecedented step of making an official response "at the highest appropriate level of authority" to a text in whose preparation some of its theologians had shared but which was nevertheless proposed to it from another body.[20] Like all other churches, the Roman Catholic Church made its own judgments on the Lima document, which were in fact encouragingly positive even while voicing some criticisms and expressing certain reservations; but the important point is that the Roman Catholic Church thus showed itself willing to participate with others in the process of elaborating and receiving and perhaps finally one day adopting in some form a statement of doctrine. If such a willingness persists

---

20. The forty-page Roman Catholic response is found in *Churches Respond to BEM: Official Responses to the "Baptism, Eucharist and Ministry" Text,* volume 6, Faith and Order Paper No. 144 (Geneva: WCC, 1988), pp. 1-40.

through the continuing Faith and Order projects on the apostolic faith, on ecclesiology, and on hermeneutics, then that can only help to break down any notion of an exercise of Rome's claimed supreme teaching office in splendid confessional isolation.[21]

Prayer

In paragraph 23, the Pope declares that "along the ecumenical path to unity, pride of place certainly belongs to common prayer, the prayerful union of those who gather together around Christ himself. If Christians, despite their divisions, can grow ever more united around Christ, they will grow in the awareness of how little divides them in comparison to what unites them. If they meet more often and more regularly before Christ in prayer, they will be able to gain the courage to face all the painful human reality of their divisions, and they will find themselves together once more in that community of the Church which Christ constantly builds up in the Holy Spirit, in spite of all weaknesses and human limitations." In paragraph 24, the pope commends especially the Week of Prayer for Christian Unity as an occasion for Christians to pray together; and it is noteworthy that since 1966, Faith and Order and the Secretariat (now Pontifical Council) for Promoting Christian Unity have been collaborating in producing materials used around the world during the Octave and on other occasions. It is no mean thing that the Roman pontiff should thereby affirm this form of *communio in sacris* as both significant of the measure of unity already enjoyed and also productive of further unity. I remember from my undergraduate days at Cambridge in the late 1950s that the only religious act allowed to Catholics and Protestants in common was the recitation of the Lord's Prayer, and even that was a recent concession for Catholics, and

21. Of the Faith and Order projects: *BEM* is by no means a dead letter, but continues to influence dialogues between the churches and liturgical revisions within them; the "apostolic faith study" proceeds by way of *Confessing the One Faith* and now an accompanying "study guide for discussion groups," *Towards Sharing the One Faith*, Faith and Order Paper No. 173 (Geneva: WCC, 1996); "ecclesiology" is at the stage represented by *The Nature and Purpose of the Church* (November 1998); and the hermeneutical study recommended from Santiago de Compestela has resulted in *A Treasure in Earthen Vessels: An Instrument for an Ecumenical Reflection on Hermeneutics*, Faith and Order Paper No. 182 (Geneva: WCC, 1998).

of course we never knew whether to go on with "For thine is the kingdom. . . ."

Unity implies and requires not only prayer *with* one another but also prayer *for* one another. The WCC's ecumenical prayer cycle includes many mentions of Roman Catholics and their church, and the theological rationale of "mutual intercession" was set out in a study by Lukas Vischer, director of Faith and Order from 1965 to 1979.[22] In terms of liturgical history, it is noteworthy that many Protestant churches, in informal practice at least, now include the bishop of Rome in their prayers, for the inclusion or omission of names among the "diptychs" was traditionally a sign of ecclesial communion or its absence. The potential of this "lex orandi" practice for the "lex credendi" merits consideration.

Baptism

In paragraph 42 of his encyclical the pope recalls, with a footnoted mention of Faith and Order's *BEM,* that "the fundamental role of baptism in building up the Church has been clearly brought out thanks also to multilateral dialogues," and he endorses "the hope that baptisms will be mutually and officially recognized." Later on, in enumerating in paragraph 66 the elements shared by the post-Reformation churches with the Catholic Church, John Paul II quotes the Vatican II decree on ecumenism to say that "the sacrament of baptism, which we have in common, represents 'a sacramental bond of unity linking all who have been reborn by means of it.' The theological, pastoral, and ecumenical implications of our common baptism are many and important. Although this sacrament of itself is 'only a beginning, a point of departure,' it is 'oriented towards a complete profession of faith, a complete incorporation into the system of salvation such as Christ himself willed it to be, and finally, towards a complete participation in Eucharistic communion.'" Certainly, the Roman Catholic Church, along with many Anglicans and Lutherans in particular, have considered a presumed "common baptism" to be fundamental to their ecumenism, but the premise of a common baptism has never been fully admitted either by the Orthodox or by the Baptists. A Faith and Order consultation held at Faverges, France, in January 1997, came reluctantly to admit that a *petitio*

22. Lukas Vischer, *Intercession* (Geneva: WCC, 1980).

principii may be involved in certain cases: "In worship at the Fifth World Conference on Faith and Order delegates affirmed and celebrated together 'the increasing mutual recognition of one another's baptism as the one baptism into Christ.' Indeed such an affirmation has become fundamental for the churches' participation in the ecumenical movement. Yet the situation is complex, and sometimes more difficult than expected. It is not always clear precisely what is being 'recognized,' especially when the recognition of baptism does not mean admission to the table of the Lord. And of course there continue to be churches, including some deeply committed to the ecumenical quest, who in fact do *not* recognize the baptism administered by others."[23] Obviously, this is a matter on which, as they say, "further work is needed."

Eucharist

In paragraph 45, which contains a footnoted reference to *BEM* and to worship services at the Vancouver and Canberra Assemblies of the WCC and the Santiago Conference of Faith and Order, the pope remarks on liturgical renewal within and among the various churches and sees it as indicative of sacramental convergence between them and the Catholic Church. Implicitly, the Roman pontiff recognizes the efficacy of the Eucharist — both word and sacrament — also in churches other than his own to advance the unity of all Christians. Surely this is a further sign, from the highest level, of a development in Roman Catholic ecclesiology that is struggling to find a theologically responsible way of admitting the ecclesial character of other Christian communities without forfeiting — though in some sense modifying — its own self-understanding. The remarkable passage reads as follows:

> Corresponding to the liturgical renewal carried out by the Catholic Church, certain other Ecclesial Communities have made efforts to re-

---

23. *Becoming a Christian: The Ecumenical Implications of our Common Baptism*, Paper F0/97:13 revised, pp. 36f. (paragraph 68). The text is printed also in *Studia Liturgica* 29 (1999), pp. 1-28, here p. 26. The difficulties come out in the papers from a consultation held in Hvittorp, Finland, in 1996 by the Lutheran Institute for Ecumenical Research, Strasbourg; see *Baptism and the Unity of the Church*, ed. Risto Saarinen and Michael Root (Grand Rapids: Eerdmans, 1998).

new their worship. Some, on the basis of a recommendation expressed at the ecumenical level [i.e. *BEM*, "Eucharist," 30-31], have abandoned the custom of celebrating their liturgy of the Lord's Supper only infrequently and have opted for a celebration each Sunday. Again, when the cycles of liturgical readings used by the various Christian Communities in the West are compared, they appear to be essentially the same. Still on the ecumenical level, very special prominence has been given to the liturgy and liturgical signs (images, icons, vestments, light, incense, gestures). Moreover, in schools of theology where future ministers are trained, courses in the history and significance of the liturgy are beginning to be part of the curriculum in response to a newly discovered need.

These are signs of convergence which regard various aspects of the sacramental life. Certainly, due to disagreements in matters of faith, it is not yet possible to celebrate together the same Eucharistic Liturgy. And yet we do have a burning desire to join in celebrating the one Eucharist of the Lord, and this desire itself is already a common prayer of praise, a single supplication. Together we speak to the Father and increasingly we do so "with one heart." At times it seems that we are closer to being able finally to seal this "real although not yet full" communion. A century ago who could even have imagined such a thing?

In paragraph 79, the short list of "areas in need of fuller study before a true consensus of faith can be achieved" includes "the Eucharist, as the sacrament of the Body and Blood of Christ, an offering of praise to the Father, the sacrificial memorial and Real Presence of Christ, and the sanctifying outpouring of the Holy Spirit" — all themes on which *BEM* and the churches' responses record considerable progress.

Visible Unity

In paragraph 77 of *Ut Unum Sint*, the pope roundly declares that "the ultimate goal of the ecumenical movement is to re-establish full visible unity among all the baptized," continuing in the next paragraph with "it is not only the Catholic Church and the Orthodox Churches which hold to this demanding concept of the unity willed by God. The orientation towards such unity is also expressed by others." A footnote reads, "The steady work of the Commission on Faith and Order has led to a comparable vision adopted by the Seventh Assembly of the World Council of Churches in the Canberra Declaration (7-20 February 1991); cf. *Signs of the Spirit,* Seventh Assembly, WCC, Geneva, 1991, pp. 235-258. This vision was reaffirmed by the World Conference of Faith and Order at Santiago de Compostela (3-14 August 1993)." An unremitting attachment to the visibility of unity will remain imperative in face of the perennial temptation to docetism or gnosticism and the current danger of acquiescence in the postmodern mood of fragmentation.

Scripture, Tradition, and Magisterium

One of the most remarkable phrasings in the entire encyclical is the pope's choice of terms to state the need for fuller study on — note the formulation — "the relationship between Sacred Scripture, as *the highest authority in matters of faith,* and Sacred Tradition, as *indispensable to the interpretation of the Word of God.*" No other way of putting the matter offers such promise of allowing the principled settlement of a controversy that has divided Protestants and Catholics since the sixteenth century. Much groundwork had been laid — unmentioned by the pope — in the World Conference of Faith and Order at Montreal in 1963 and its statement on "Scripture, Tradition and traditions." The conference recognized Scripture as the canonical testimony to the gospel and therefore as the internal norm of the one Tradition — which is "Christ himself present in the life of the Church" — and the criterion for determining the authenticity of particular communal traditions. Yet Montreal itself realized that the question of the *interpretation* of Scripture — i.e., the question of the modes and agents of its interpretation — was not thereby settled. That realization led Faith and Order first to work further on "authoritative teaching" — "How Does the Church Teach Authoritatively Today?" — and then to heed the cry at Santiago for an "ecumenical hermeneutics."[24] The report made so far on the latter project — *A Treasure in Earthen Vessels* — acknowledges that within "the Church as an hermeneutical community" there is need for a "ministry of oversight" in this respect also, and notes with approval the in-

24. A survey of the earlier work is included with the up-to-date results from post-Santiago efforts in *A Treasure in Earthen Vessels: An Instrument for an Ecumenical Reflection on Hermeneutics,* Faith and Order Paper No. 182 (Geneva: WCC, 1998).

stances of its collegial exercise, which in some parts of the world functions even as "shared oversight on matters of Christian faith and witness by churches who are not yet visibly united." The report adds, moreover, that "the ecumenical movement considers its dialogues and preliminary structures of deliberation and consultation to be not only instruments for the fulfillment of its hermeneutical task but also a patient preparation for coming together in a genuine ecumenical council able to restore full *koinonia* as God wills."[25] Still, the report gives no evidence of having faced the Roman claim contained in what John Paul II lists in paragraph 79 among the areas in need of fuller study, namely "the Magisterium of the Church, entrusted to the Pope and the Bishops in communion with him, understood as a responsibility and an authority exercised in the name of Christ for teaching and safeguarding the faith." One strand to explore might be the whole process — the preparation, accomplishment, authorization, reception, and use — associated with ecumenical translations of the Scriptures. The pope highlighted the importance of these translations in paragraph 44 of the encyclical: "Significant progress in ecumenical cooperation has also been made in another area, that of the Word of God. I am thinking above all of the importance for different language groups of ecumenical translations of the Bible. Following the promulgation by the Second Vatican Council of the Constitution *Dei Verbum,* the Catholic Church could not fail to welcome this development. These translations, prepared by experts, generally offer a solid basis for the prayer and pastoral activity of all Christ's followers. Anyone who recalls how heavily debates about Scripture influenced divisions, especially in the West, can appreciate the significant step forward which these common translations represent."

The Virgin Mary

The last of the "areas in need of fuller study" listed by Pope John Paul II in paragraph 79 of his encyclical is "the Virgin Mary, as Mother of God and Icon of the Church, the Spiritual Mother who intercedes for Christ's disciples and for all humanity." Marian piety and doctrines are themselves matters for substantial ecumenical exploration. The question of the Petrine ministry comes particularly into play, however, by virtue of the fact that

25. *A Treasure in Earthen Vessels,* pp. 33-41 (paragraphs 49-66).

the dogmatic promulgation of Mary's Immaculate Conception (1854) and Assumption (1950) constitute the two most dramatic instances of the apparent exercise of an extraordinary magisterium by the bishop of Rome.

Saints and Martyrs

"In a theocentric vision," writes the pope in paragraph 84, "we Christians already have a common *Martyrology*," which "shows how, at a profound level, God preserves communion among the baptized in the supreme demand of faith, manifested in the sacrifice of life itself." "Albeit in an invisible way," he continues, "the communion between our Communities, even if still incomplete, is grounded in the full communion of the Saints — those who, at the end of a life faithful to grace, are in communion with Christ in glory. These *Saints* come from all the Churches and Ecclesial Communities which gave them entrance into the communion of salvation. . . . In the radiance of the 'heritage of the saints' belonging to all Communities, the 'dialogue of conversion' towards full and visible unity thus appears as a source of hope. This universal presence of the Saints is in fact a proof of the transcendent power of the Spirit. It is the sign and proof of God's victory over the forces which divide humanity." May I suggest that the pope would be exercising, in his pastoral capacity, a universal ministry of unity if he were to give calendrical and liturgical recognition by name to certain men and women who are also viewed as saints by those other Christian communities, in the bosom of which they bore the witness of faith in a conspicuous and exemplary manner?[26]

The Petrine Office

In paragraph 88, John Paul II recalls that on a visit to the WCC in Geneva in 1984 he acknowledged that "the Catholic Church's conviction that in the ministry of the Bishop of Rome she has preserved, in fidelity to the Apostolic Tradition and the faith of the Fathers, the visible sign and guarantor of unity, constitutes a difficulty for most other Christians, whose mem-

---

26. See the arguments presented in Geoffrey Wainwright, *Methodists in Dialogue* (Nashville: Abingdon Press, 1995), pp. 237-249 ("Wesley and the Communion of Saints").

ory is marked by certain painful recollections." He now finds it encouraging that "the question of the primacy of the Bishop of Rome" should have been taken up not only in bilateral dialogues involving Rome and others, but also in the recommendation of the Santiago Conference of Faith and Order to begin a study on "the question of a universal ministry of Christian unity," the first hints of which we have already discussed in the first half of this paper.

The pope also briefly rehearses the place and roles of Peter in the New Testament. Recognizing that a Petrine ministry must always be exercised as the *servus servorum Dei,* in episcopal collegiality and within the communion of the faithful, he summarizes the responsibilities of "the Successor of Peter" in this way in paragraph 94:

> With the power and the authority without which such an office would be illusory, the Bishop of Rome must ensure the communion of all the churches. For this reason, he is the first servant of unity. This primacy is exercised on various levels, including vigilance over the handing down of the Word, the celebration of the Liturgy and the Sacraments, the Church's mission, discipline and the Christian life. It is the responsibility of the Successor of Peter to recall the requirements of the common good of the Church, should anyone be tempted to overlook it in the pursuit of personal interests. He has the duty to admonish, to caution, and to declare at times that this or that opinion being circulated is irreconcilable with the unity of faith. When circumstances require it, he speaks in the name of all the Pastors in communion with him. He can also — under very specific conditions clearly laid down by the First Vatican Council — declare *ex cathedra* that a certain doctrine belongs to the deposit of faith. By thus bearing witness to the truth, he serves unity.

John Paul II concludes the section by asking, "Do not many of those involved in ecumenism today feel a need for such a ministry? A ministry which presides in truth and love so that the ship — that beautiful symbol which the World Council of Churches has chosen as its emblem — will not be buffeted by the storms and will one day reach its haven." It is in that light that he calls, in paragraph 96, for "a patient and fraternal dialogue," of which the present conference is at least indirectly a part. Among Protestants this invitation is most likely to appeal to those participants in the ecumenical movement who, along the classic lines of Faith and Order, have looked for the restoration of ecclesial unity on the basis of Scripture and the common Tradition but now fear that more recent developments in Protestantism lead away from that basis and goal. They — I should in candor say we — may now, since the proven entry of the Roman Catholic Church into the ecumenical movement, consider the offer of a Roman magisterium as conceivably the best safeguard against the increasing dissolution of our own Protestant tradition(s).

Unity and Evangelization

In a couple of passionate paragraphs (98-99) toward the end of the encyclical, Pope John Paul II recaptures the original "inspiration and guiding motif" of the modern ecumenical movement, its "missionary outlook." Recalling, of course, that the doxological thrust of Jesus' prayer in John 17 sets "the glory of the Father" as the ultimate goal of unity, the pope indicates that the immediate purpose of the petition *"ut unum sint"* is *"ut mundus credat."* "The lack of unity among Christians," the Pope sees, "contradicts the Truth which Christians have the mission to spread and, consequently, it gravely damages their witness." "How," he asks, "can we proclaim the Gospel of reconciliation without at the same time being committed to working for reconciliation between Christians?" Since lack of unity infringes "the fundamental law of love," the "imperative of charity" means that "ecumenism is not only an internal question of the Christian Communities"; rather, the Pope declares, "it is a matter of the love which God has in Jesus Christ for all humanity; to stand in the way of this love is an offense against him and against his plan to gather all people in Christ." The implicit challenge here to Faith and Order is that it should help the World Council of Churches as a whole heed the calls of Orthodox and Evangelicals at least since the Canberra Assembly of 1991 to return to the interrelated concerns for mission and unity that originally drove the modern ecumenical movement.[27] Whether that can be managed inside the existing structures and composition of the WCC remains a matter for thought, prayer, and action.[28]

27. See *Signs of the Spirit: Official Report, Seventh Assembly, Canberra, Australia, 7-20 February 1991*, ed. Michael Kinnamon (Geneva: WCC; Grand Rapids: Eerdmans, 1991), pp. 279-286.
28. See Geoffrey Wainwright, "Faith and Order within or without the World Council of Churches" in *The Ecumenical Review* 45 (1993): 118-121.

Corresponding to the pope's concluding challenge to ecumenists (which in principle means all Christians), I will close with an oblique address to any twenty-first century holder of a Petrine ministry, such as can be found in the exposition of John 21 by a great advocate of mission and unity in the twentieth century, namely the late Lesslie Newbigin, bishop in the Church of South India:

> In the first part [of the chapter] Peter is the fisherman who (if only he is obedient to the Lord) is able to catch not only a vast number of fish, but also (unlike the so-called evangelists who leave as their legacy a litter of mutually competing sects) is able to bring them all to the feet of Jesus as one, with no "schism" in the net (John 21:11). Then Peter is the shepherd to whom the Lord entrusts his sheep, but only because he is assured that Peter loves Him, the one to whom the sheep belong. But finally — and this is where the chapter comes to its crucial point — Peter is a disciple. The words "Follow me," in the context of all that has gone before (see 13:36-38), constitute the punch-line of the whole chapter. But this decisive word can only be spoken because Peter has learned what following means — not his own program, but the way of the Cross (21:18f.). Peter in other words can be a shepherd only if he is a disciple. He can bring others to Jesus and guard them in His ownership only if he is himself following Jesus on the way of the Cross. He can be a leader only as he is a follower — a follower on the way of the Cross. Following Jesus on the way of the Cross in such wise that others are enabled to follow: this, I believe, is the heart of what the New Testament has to say about ministry.[29]

Epilogue

Since my own Methodist tradition was not explicitly included in the program of this conference, perhaps I will now mention a few recent refer-

29. The quotation comes from a paper entitled simply "Ministry" and dated "late 1980s," which is lodged in box 9 of the Newbigin archive at the Selly Oak Colleges Library, Birmingham. In that same paper, in connection with "the right balance of personal and conciliar elements in the government of the Church at every level — local, regional, national, universal," Newbigin wrote: "That means that Protestants have to take seriously the Roman Catholic witness about primacy, that Catholics have to take seriously the testimony of Protestants about the role of the church meeting and the synod or council." My book *Lesslie Newbigin: A Theological Life* was published by Oxford University Press in the spring of 2000.

ences that have been made from within Methodism to the question of a Petrine ministry, first from the official dialogue between the World Methodist Council and the Roman Catholic Church, and then a couple of individual responses to *Ut Unum Sint*. The Honolulu 1981 report, *Towards an Agreed Statement on the Holy Spirit*, contained, in extract, the following sentences as part of a discussion of authority in the church:

> We believe that emotions surrounding such relatively modern terms as infallibility and irreformability can be diminished if they are looked at in the light of our shared doctrine concerning the Holy Spirit. The papal authority, no less than any other within the Church, is a manifestation of the continuing presence of the Spirit of love in the Church or it is nothing. Indeed it should in its exercise be preeminently such a manifestation. . . . The terms [infallibility and universal and immediate jurisdiction] are to be understood in light of the total conception and the total responsibility of teaching and disciplinary office in the Church — a pastoral office mirroring the constant presence and solicitude of the Spirit within the Church, leading into truth and disciplining in love. . . . The general idea of a universal service of unity within the Church, a primacy of charity mirroring the presence and work in the Church of the Spirit who is love, may well be a basis for increased understanding and convergence.

The Nairobi report of 1986, *Towards a Statement on the Church*, tackled in some detail, though no doubt prematurely, the theme of the Petrine office. The most noticed sentences in the thirty-seven relevant paragraphs are these: "Methodists accept that what is properly required for the unity of the whole of Christ's Church must by that very fact be God's will for his Church. A universal primacy might well serve as focus of, and ministry for the unity of the whole Church" (paragraph 58); and: "It would not be inconceivable that at some future date in a restored unity, Roman Catholic and Methodist bishops might be linked in one episcopal college, and that the whole body would recognize some kind of effective leadership and primacy in the bishop of Rome. In that case Methodists might justify such acceptance on different grounds from those that now prevail in the Roman Catholic Church" (paragraph 62).[30] The 1991 Singapore report on *The Ap-*

30. The Honolulu and earlier reports can be found in *Growth in Agreement: Reports and Agreements of Ecumenical Conversations on a World Level,* ed. Harding Meyer and Lukas

ostolic Tradition and the 1996 Rio de Janeiro report entitled *The Word of Life: A Statement on Revelation and Faith* both move toward some common perspectives on fundamental matters related to Petrine ministry. The current series of talks comes closer with an examination of teaching authority in the church.

Of the two individual contributions, the first comes from Walter Klaiber, a New Testament scholar and bishop of the Evangelisch-methodistische Kirche in Germany (a conference of the United Methodist Church). He contributed an article to the Tübingen Catholic review *Theologische Quartalschrift,* in an issue entitled "Die ökumenische Zukunft des Petrusdienstes" that brought together reactions to the papal encyclical from various ecclesial traditions.[31] As a bishop, Klaiber admits the weakness of the teaching office in Methodism as in Protestantism generally and, more positively, he notes the existence of a college of bishops in the United Methodist Church that meets annually under a presidency that, admittedly, changes by the year. As a *Neutestamentler,* Klaiber recognizes in the scriptural texts a *"Verständnispotential"* for a continuing Petrine ministry; but as a theologian, he believes that "potential" would have to be judged not in light of the factual historical development over the centuries but rather in light of the total message of Jesus; and as a practical ecumenist, he wonders whether the "monumentality" of the existing papal office would not prevent the development of a differently conceived Petrine ministry. Klaiber is not opposed to the idea of an interdenominational office of pastoral service to other servant pastors, but suggests that it might be more effective at a regional rather than a universal level. He is aware that Pope John II wishes to heed the request made of him — in accordance with "the ecumenical aspirations of the majority of the Christian communities" — "to find a way of exercising the primacy which, while in no way renouncing what is essential to its mission, is nonetheless open to a

---

Vischer (Ramsey, N.J.: Paulist Press, and Geneva: WCC, 1984), and the Nairobi, Singapore, and Rio de Janeiro reports in *Deepening Communion: International Ecumenical Documents with Roman Catholic Participation,* ed. William G. Rusch and Jeffrey Gros (Washington, D.C.: United States Catholic Conference, 1998). That the Roman see itself has advanced historically various justifications for its claims is shown by Klaus Schatz, *Papal Primacy: From Its Origins to the Present* (Collegeville, Minn.: Liturgical Press, 1996).

31. Walter Klaiber, "Die Einheit der Kirche und der Wille Gottes — Evangelisch-methodistisches Positionspapier zum Gespräch über den Primat des Papstes," *Theologische Quartalschrift* 178 (1998): 131-140.

new situation" (*Ut Unum Sint*, paragraph 95). Klaiber finishes by wondering just how much *"Spielraum"* that leaves for a genuine rapprochement.

The other individual contribution is one that I myself made to a symposium organized by the Society of the Atonement in Rome in December 1997 under the title "Petrine Ministry and the Unity of the Church." There I argued that Methodism's receptivity to the paired biblical themes of "truth and love" renders it open to discussion of such a doctrinal and pastoral ministry, and that our structural "connexionalism" and our traditional ministerial "itinerancy" makes familiar the notion of a ministry to facilitate the circulation of love and truth in the Body of Christ. I wondered whether Pope John Paul II's words in paragraph 94 of *Ut Unum Sint* about a very particular gift and responsibility given to *one* among the bishops of the church might be accepted in the framework of what Methodists sing more generally in a hymn about mutual love and consensus in the truth:

> The gift which He on one bestows,
> We all delight to prove.

In conclusion I offered a personal suggestion, which met with interest at the time and has attracted some attention since, and with which I again conclude:

> My respectful suggestion is that the Pope should invite those Christian communities which he regards as being in real, if imperfect, communion with the Roman Catholic Church to appoint representatives to cooperate with him and his appointees in formulating a statement expressive of the Gospel to be preached to the world today. Thus the theme of the "fraternal dialogue" which John Paul II envisaged would shift from the *theory* of the pastoral and doctrinal office to the *substance* of what is believed and preached. And the very *exercise* of elaborating a statement of faith might — by the process of its launching, its execution, its resultant form, its publication, and its reception — illuminate the question of "a ministry that presides in truth and love." *Solvitur ambulando.*[32]

---

32. Geoffrey Wainwright, "'The Gift Which He on One Bestows, We All Delight to Prove': A Possible Methodist Approach to a Ministry of Primacy in the Circulation of Love and Truth," in *Petrine Ministry and the Unity of the Church*, ed. James F. Puglisi (Collegeville, Minn.: Liturgical Press, 1999), pp. 59-82; quote, p. 82.

The Papal Office and the Burdens of History: A Lutheran View

DAVID S. YEAGO

I have been asked to respond as a Lutheran to the generous invitation of Pope John Paul II that is the occasion for this conference. In doing so, I want to avoid attempting to reinvent the wheel and so will take as my starting point the two most significant ecumenical dialogues in which Lutherans and Roman Catholics have already discussed the papacy together: rounds five and six of the Lutheran-Roman Catholic dialogue in the United States, which produced the volumes *Papal Primacy and the Universal Church* and *Teaching Authority and Infallibility in the Church*.[1] These volumes are now twenty-five and twenty years old, respectively, but it cannot be said that the reports they contain have had their day. On the contrary, in both churches the reception of these reports has been quite partial and fragmentary, in some contrast to the statements of the same dialogue on Eucharist and justification, which have been far more influential in shaping informed opinion in both communions.

This has some basis in the dialogue texts themselves, which I have come to think are difficult texts in a way in which those on Eucharist and justification are not. But this difficulty in the texts is grounded in the dis-

---

1. Paul C. Empie and T. Austin Murphy, eds., *Papal Primacy and the Universal Church.* Lutherans and Catholics in Dialogue V (Minneapolis: Augsburg, 1974); Paul C. Empie, T. Austin Murphy, and Joseph A. Burgess, eds., *Teaching Authority and Infallibility in the Church.* Lutherans and Catholics in Dialogue VI (Minneapolis: Augsburg, 1978, 1980); hereafter referred to as *PPUC* and *TAIC,* respectively.

tinctive difficulty of the ecumenical problem that they address. For with the papacy, if anywhere, it becomes clear that ecumenism is never simply a matter of the dialectical reconciliation of differing structures of thought in a more complex synthesis. Rather, ecumenism seeks the reconciliation of actual space-time communities, communities which exist *in* history and *through* history, even as they proclaim and experience the inaugurated consummation of history in the eucharistic foretaste of the reign of God. The ecumenical task is therefore never simply a conceptual task; it is an irreducibly political task, insofar as it involves persuasion and action with a view to shaping the common life of historically particular human communities. It calls not only for dialectical skill but for a kind of eschatological statecraft, a distinctive sort of political wisdom and resolve appropriate to the public life of a people whose commonwealth is in heaven.[2]

Like all politics, moreover, ecumenical politics has to deal with the burdens of history, with the mass and momentum of social bodies, and with the accumulation of memories, the patterns of behavior, and the heritage of attitudes and passions objectified therein. Perhaps the distinctive lesson of the second Christian millennium has been the harsh discovery that the church is no less liable to accumulate such burdens than the nations. Despite the presence within the church of the reconciling consummation of history, the church is no less capable than the nations of becoming frozen in irreconcilable oppositions. It will doubtless be among the main challenges of the third millennium to reflect more deeply and adequately on this dark enigma. Even more, it will be the task of Christians in the decades and centuries to come to ask more radically than we have before what the disciplines of personal and communal life might promise, as instruments of the Spirit, to break the hold of the passions that divide the mind and heart of the Christian people.

This paper will contribute only indirectly to those ends, yet it is necessary to evoke such larger issues as the context in which we may most fruitfully take a new look at the U.S. dialogue statements on papal primacy and magisterium. No other locus of Christian disunity is so burdened by

2. It needs to be emphasized, therefore, that when this essay speaks of "political" aspects of the ecumenical problem, and of the "politics" of the church, it is not referring to something disreputable about which one might well be cynical. The church is properly and necessarily a political community, even a supremely political community, insofar as it must engage in deliberation, debate, and decision about its movement through history toward its goal.

history as the papacy; the Holy Father spoke with what can only be called delicate understatement when he said that ". . . the Catholic Church's conviction that in the ministry of the Bishop of Rome she has preserved . . . the visible sign and guarantor of unity, constitutes a difficulty for most other Christians, whose memory is marked by certain painful recollections."[3] To this we can only reply, "You're not kidding."

The difficulty of the texts to which we now turn is precisely the tacit struggle with the burdens of history that occurs in the midst and around the edges of their theological reformulations. That struggle is only partly acknowledged and explicit in the texts,[4] yet the logic of significant moves and departures becomes clear only when we recognize the struggle behind the scenes.

A Functional Account of Papal Primacy

The 1974 Report of the U.S. Dialogue on Papal Primacy announces that it did not reach full agreement by its very title: "Differing Attitudes to Papal Primacy." This title already betrays, no doubt, the felt pressure of the burdens of history, for nothing in the statement itself would forbid calling it "Converging Perspectives on Papal Primacy" or something else more typically optimistic. The dialogue in fact made significant progress; it succeeded in identifying a framework of thought within which, after centuries of mutual suspicion and denunciation, a reasoned theological discussion of primacy could take place. That is a remarkable achievement all by itself. That the dialogue team was unable to carry through to the end the conversation thus initiated was certainly no failure.

The first major section of the "Common Statement" on papal primacy is entitled "The Setting of the Problem" and it is here that this dialogue's greatest contribution is made. In the previous history of conflict over the papacy, the most common "setting of the problem" was the opposition of rights and claims. The Roman Church and its bishop claimed by divine right certain powers of supervision and direction over the churches

---

3. *Ut Unum Sint*, No. 88.

4. Cf. the introduction to the "Common Statement" in *PPUC* for a general acknowledgment of this dimension of the problem: "the role of the papacy has been the subject of intense controversy, which has generated theological disagreements, organizational differences, and psychological antagonisms" (p. 9).

throughout the world, and these claims were in turn opposed, at various times and places, but with increasing vehemence in the second millennium, first in the East and then in the separated churches of the West, as mere human imposture and power-seeking. The theological contestation of the issue devolved into what was essentially the preparation of a series of briefs, in which Scripture and the Fathers were combed for arguments for and against what came to be called "The Roman Claims." Long before the beginning of the modern ecumenical movement, every shred of possible evidence had been gathered and organized into mutually contradictory systems of interpretation and argument. Clearly the greatest need, if dialogue on primacy was to be possible at all, was precisely a new way of locating the problem.

Drawing on earlier theological and ecumenical work,[5] the U.S. dialogue located primacy within just such a new horizon: the *mission* of the church. In this sense one can say that it provides a functional account of primacy as common ground for dialogue — not functional as in "nontheological," but rather as in "sociological-pragmatic," because what is at stake is an understanding of primacy within the drama of the church's apostolic mission, given by Jesus Christ. The opening paragraph of this first major section of the "Common Statement" sets the stage and deserves to be cited extensively:

> The church as reconciled and reconciling community cannot serve God's purpose in the world as it should when its own life is torn by divisions and disagreements. The members of the church, wherever they are found, are part of a single people, the one body of Christ, whose mission is to be an anticipatory and efficacious sign of the final unification of all things when God will be all in all. In order to bear credible witness to this coming kingdom, the various Christian bodies must mutually assist

5. Chiefly the report of the international Joint Lutheran–Roman Catholic Study Commission on "The Gospel and the Church," known as the "Malta Report"; cf. Harding Meyer and Lukas Vischer, eds., *Growth in Agreement: Reports and Agreed Statements of Ecumenical Conversations on a World Level* (New York: Paulist Press; Geneva: World Council of Churches, 1984), pp. 168-189. The study commission that produced the Malta Report shared two members with the U.S. dialogue team that produced "Differing Attitudes towards Papal Primacy": the Roman Catholic biblical scholar Joseph Fitzmeyer and (on this particular issue, doubtless the most significant link) the Lutheran theologian George A. Lindbeck. Lindbeck's landmark essay in *PPUC*, "Papacy and Ius Divinum: A Lutheran View" (pp. 193-208), clarifies abundantly the conceptual links between the two reports.

and correct each other and must collaborate in all matters which concern the mission and welfare of the church universal.[6]

This mission perspective is the starting point from which the report develops its crucial notion of the "Petrine function," defined as "a particular form of Ministry exercised by a person, officeholder, or local church with reference to the church as a whole."

> This Petrine function of the Ministry serves to promote or preserve the oneness of the church by symbolizing unity, and by facilitating communication, mutual assistance or correction, and collaboration in the church's mission."[7]

The Petrine *function,* so described, is not identical with the Petrine *primacy* claimed by the pope; it is really a function of all Christian ministry, which is in every case concerned with the one church and its one mission. The notion of a "Petrine function" of Christian ministry serves as a context, however, within which to redescribe and reconsider the idea of Petrine primacy. In this perspective, the distinctive role in the universal church claimed by the pope can be understood as a special concentration of the Petrine function of the ministry. The pope is therefore not in the first instance a sovereign invested with supreme power, but a pastor called to a crucially important concretion of a necessary task of Christian ministry. That is, the pope is called in a special, though not exclusive, way "to promote or preserve the oneness of the church by symbolizing unity, and by facilitating communication, mutual assistance or correction, and collaboration in the church's mission." Papal *power* can therefore be considered in subordination to this papal *ministry;* it can be described, in the precise phrase of Pope John Paul II, as "the power and the authority without which such an office would be illusory."[8]

The older way of putting the question left little scope for theological discussion: either Jesus Christ did or he did not confer on Peter supreme authority over the whole church in such a way as to found a continuing plenary jurisdiction. The mode of argument is, in a sense, positivistic; the question reduces itself to whether competent authority has indeed man-

6. *PPUC,* p. 10.
7. *PPUC,* p. 11; italics in original.
8. *Ut Unum Sint,* No. 94.

dated this particular arrangement of power. Once sides have been taken and the evidence presented, there is really nothing more to discuss; we can only wait for the Last Day, when the court will presumably render its verdict.

The central theological achievement of the U.S. dialogue was to relocate the issue of primacy in a teleological context, within which we can ask what good the primacy of Rome might serve, in what ways, and under what conditions. Since other Christians generally agree with Catholics that Christian ministry does have a "Petrine function" in the sense described, dialogue is indeed possible. One can ask whether it would be legitimate and helpful for the Petrine function of the ministry to receive a special concentration of this sort. One can ask what reasons there are for locating such a Petrine ministry precisely in the local church of Rome and its bishop. One can discuss just what power and authority really are required "lest such an office be illusory," and to what degree the concrete ways in which the office has been exercised have helped or hindered its fulfillment of its task. The claim of divine institution need by no means be surrendered, but its force is altered when the function of papal primacy in a teleology of mission becomes central evidence for it.

This theological relocation of the ecumenical problem of primacy is undoubtedly the most widely received aspect of the 1974 report; the dialogue has succeeded in generating a new discussion of papal primacy on new lines between Catholics and Lutherans.[9] The degree to which this approach to the question of papal primacy has been received in the churches is perhaps best illustrated by the way in which the pope himself uses it in *Ut Unum Sint:*

> The first part of the Acts of the Apostles presents Peter as the one who speaks in the name of the apostolic group and who serves the unity of the community, all the while respecting the authority of James, the head of the Church in Jerusalem. This function of Peter must continue in the Church so that under her sole Head, who is Jesus Christ, she may be visibly present in the world as the communion of all his disciples. Do not many of those involved in ecumenism today feel a need for such a ministry? A ministry which presides in truth and love so that the ship . . . will not be buffeted by the storms and will one day reach its haven.[10]

9. And not only among Catholics and Lutherans: the two reports of the first Anglican–Roman Catholic International Commission (ARIC) on "Authority in the Church" (1976, 1981) follow a similar line. Cf. *Growth in Agreement,* pp. 88-117.

10. *Ut Unum Sint,* No. 97-98.

There are striking parallels between this passage and the paragraph in which the U.S. dialogue report introduces the notion of the Petrine function.[11] In both there is an evocation of New Testament presentations of Peter's role in the apostolic company, followed by the suggestion that also in the church today there may be need of such a ministry. The pope's explicitly functional presentation of his office is indeed the basis for the invitation to which we have gathered to respond: "that we may seek — together, of course — the forms in which this ministry may accomplish a service of love recognized by all concerned."[12]

Lutheran reflection on the idea of a special Petrine ministry for the whole church has continued since 1974, and it has become clear in the interim that an even stronger Lutheran case for such ministry can be made than appears in the dialogue report. For the main tradition of Lutheran ecclesiology, the relationship of shepherd and flock, pastor and people, is structurally essential to the form of the church's life in history. This is because the church is *creatura verbi,* created by the holy gospel of Christ, and as Peter Brunner wrote, "the gospel cannot come on the scene at all without its concrete human bearer."[13] The church as a concrete historical phenomenon is therefore irreducibly the assembly called together by apostolic messengers, the flock gathered and held in one by the ministry of shepherds. As Luther himself put it, ". . . the church cannot exist without . . . bishops, pastors, preachers, and priests, and in turn they cannot exist without the church: they must be together with one another."[14]

If this *Gegenüber* of pastor and people is an essential, concrete form of the church's ontologically crucial dependence on the gospel, we can then say that in whatever way the church's communion takes concrete form in history, it always does so in some analogical reiteration of the relationship of shepherd and flock. The church exists, for Lutheran ecclesiology, in the basic form of worshiping assemblies presided over by pastors. If the church is also to exist concretely as a communion of such assemblies, then that communion will also take form as a flock with a shepherd. It will be historically actual as a real ecclesial community insofar as it is gathered

11. *PPUC,* pp. 11-12.
12. *Ut Unum Sint,* No. 95, citing words originally addressed to the Ecumenical Patriarch Demetrios I.
13. Peter Brunner, "Sacerdotium und Ministerium," in *Bemühungen um die einigende Wahrheit* (Göttingen: Vandenhoeck & Ruprecht, 1977), p. 132.
14. Weimar Edition of Luther's Works, *Weimarer Ausgabe,* 50:641.

by a pastor who speaks the word of God to it. Obviously "gathering" must be taken analogically; the churches in a region are not "gathered into one" in the same way as a local congregation, which can physically assemble in one room.[15] Yet if "gathering" means in ecclesiology "giving concrete historical form," then one can say that the church is always "gathered" by the word addressed to it by an apostolic messenger.

But what applies to the worshiping assembly and to the communion of churches in a region must also apply to the church universal. Lutheran ecclesiology would seem therefore to imply that also the universal communion of the church can be historically actual only if there is a universal pastorate, some ministry to speak the word of God to the whole people of God on earth and so to "gather" the faithful into one concrete historical *communio,* as a foretaste of the great assembly around the throne of God and of the Lamb. Also the universal church must be *creatura verbi,* called into actuality by the word of God, a word which must be spoken by a "concrete human bearer." It is therefore possible to see a statement of Pope John Paul II cited above as a conclusion of strictly *Lutheran* theology: "This function of Peter must continue in the Church so that under her sole Head, who is Jesus Christ, she may be visibly present in the world as the communion of all his disciples."[16]

Furthermore, Wolfhart Pannenberg is surely right to argue that we should not conclude from this line of reasoning that since the church needs an office of universal pastor, we should set out to invent one. Rather, we should acknowledge that the church has already been given such an office in the special role that the bishop of Rome does actually play, whether we like it or not, in the world Christian community, and we should devote our energies to reforming his office to fulfill its purpose

---

15. It is at this point that, in a fuller discussion of this issue, answer would have to be made to those Lutherans who have argued that the translocal oversight of the churches can and should be placed in the hands of a "synod" with lay representation, rather than in the hands of a bishop. What has been said in no way militates against the possibility that such synods might play a crucial role in the governance of the church. But this only pushes the problem back a step. Who will speak the gospel precisely to the synod, so that it might be a representative assembly of the church and therefore be capable of making decisions on behalf of the church *as* church? Nor is there anything here that militates against the idea of lay participation in the governance of the church. Indeed, a "synod" made up entirely of the ordained would be no more capable of acting as the church than an assembly of laypeople unless gathered by the *ministerium verbi.*

16. *Ut Unum Sint,* No. 97.

more effectively.[17] As the Lutheran participants in the U.S. dialogue put it already in 1974:

> Structures invested with powerful symbolic meaning cannot be created at will. Therefore we do not anticipate that a concrete Ministry of unity to serve the church of the future will be something completely new. It will have to emerge from the renewal and restructuring of those historical forms which best nurture and express this unity.[18]

Or as Robert W. Jenson said a few years later:

> If all the great dreams came true and the unity of western Christendom could be reconstituted and in such fashion that all of the protestant objections to the medieval system were reckoned with, you would still have to have some kind of institution of this unity. And it would be silly to propose locating it anywhere but in Rome. What argument could you bring for Kansas City?[19]

It might be added that few more powerful signs of the reconciling power of Christ can be imagined than the mutual reconciliation of the papacy and those Christian communities whose tradition of fear and hatred of the papacy is so long and so deep. Christian unity without Roman primacy would in a real sense be unity without reconciliation, unity that evaded the burdens of history instead of confronting them.

That brings us to the limits of the dialogue's success. The plausibility of this whole line of thought depends on its starting point, the eschatological mission ecclesiology set forth in the resonant paragraph of the "Common Statement" cited above: "The members of the church, wherever they are found, are part of a single people, the one body of Christ, whose mission is to be an anticipatory and efficacious sign of the final unification of all things when God will be all in all." Only in the light of such an account of ecclesial identity will it be possible to understand why it might be ur-

17. Wolfhart Pannenberg, *Systematic Theology,* vol. 3 (Grand Rapids: Eerdmans, 1998), pp. 420ff.

18. *PPUC,* p. 31.

19. Robert W. Jenson, comments from the discussion of his lecture "A Lutheran Mode of Ecumenism," in Phil Schroeder, ed., *Center for the Study of Campus Ministry — Yearbook IV* (Valparaiso, Ind.: CSSM, 1981), sidebar to p. 9.

gent that the church of Jesus Christ "be *visibly* present in the world as the communion of all his disciples."

But to be ecumenically efficacious, this ecclesiology of mission has to be more than an affirmation of formal systematics; it has to become the shared self-understanding of the churches. It has to shape the hopes and fears of Christian people and make a difference in the way they envision their future. In a sense, the great and fundamental ecumenical reform would be the transition from a Christian identity defined by disagreements with other Christians, characteristic of the past five centuries in the West, to a Christian identity defined by the apostolic commission to a missionary engagement with the world.

It is by no means clear that we are very far along with this transition in any of our churches. Confessional identity, defined by opposition to other Christians, is by every measure declining as a truly formative factor, but it is not clear that a new identity formed through rediscovery of the church's eschatological mission is taking its place. In much of mainline Protestantism, at least in North America, confessional identity is being replaced by conservative and liberal group identities that seem to have deeper roots in secular culture wars than in the apostolic tradition. At the same time, Protestant loyalties are becoming more local, more focused on the single congregation, and less attached than ever to any wider Christian family. Among Roman Catholics, the polarization between progressive and conservative factions that has dominated the post–Vatican II era is likewise ecumenically sterile; neither party seems exactly haunted by the statement of Vatican II that as a consequence of the divisions among Christians, "the Church herself finds it more difficult to express in actual life her full catholicity,"[20] or to suspect that it might be relevant to the analysis of internal Roman Catholic difficulties.

This is, I believe, a crucial point — in a sense, the key point. The ecumenical problem of papal primacy is not simply a problem of theological affirmation; theological reformulation is a necessary but never sufficient condition for its resolution. The problem of papal primacy is a political problem in the fullest sense of the word: a problem which calls for deliberation and decision regarding the goods for which particular communities live, and the appropriate means by which those goods are to be pursued. Now the name for the political question as it arises in the community of

20. *Redintegratio Unitatis (Decree on Ecumenism)*, No. 4.

the church is precisely "mission," for it is essential to the church's life that we do not discover for ourselves the good our community seeks, but are "sent" by the risen Christ to pursue the specified good of his choosing. As a political problem, then, the problem of papal primacy, like the problem of disunity as a whole, is framed by the horizon of mission, and is doubtless insoluble without massive transformations of the lived sense of mission in all the separated churches. This is a point to which we shall find ourselves returning in more concrete ways as we turn now to look at certain other aspects of the U.S. dialogue statements on the papacy.

Proposals for Reform

After introducing the notion of the "Petrine function," the 1974 "Common Statement" goes on to discuss three controversial questions about the papacy in light of that function. I want to pass over the first two, despite their intrinsic importance, in order to devote somewhat more extended attention to the third. While the first two issues have to do with the scriptural legitimacy of a universal ministry of unity and its divine institution, the third "centers on the practical consequences drawn from these prior disagreements." Roman Catholics, according to the report, have tended to suppose that the divine institution of the papal ministry provides warrant and legitimacy for its existing structures and modes of operation, particularly its active and controlling supervision of other Christian ministries. The report cites Vatican I, referring to its description of the pope's jurisdiction over the universal church as "supreme," "full," "ordinary," and "immediate," and then continues: "This view of the exercise of papal power has been vehemently repudiated by Lutherans and viewed by them as leading to intolerable ecclesiastical tyranny."[21]

It is worth pausing to consider this language. While mild enough within the larger history of debate on the papacy, it is rather strong for an ecumenical dialogue report, a genre usually notable for the blandness of its rhetoric. Language of "vehement repudiation" and "intolerable tyranny" reflects the burden of history that inescapably bears down on this issue. It is not enough to discuss the hermeneutics of conciliar statements and ask whether an interpretation of Vatican I is possible that does not conflict

21. *PPUC,* p. 13.

with the Lutheran confessions and vice versa. There is a deep-seated perception, not only among Lutherans, that Roman Catholic teaching on papal primacy serves essentially to justify the intolerable: the subjugation of the churches to "ecclesiastical tyranny." In the actual relations of our churches, the perception of the Roman primacy as a tyrannical power is a far more consequential barrier than any set of purely conceptual objections.[22] The problem is at bottom political, because "tyranny" is a political concept.

The report makes a striking acknowledgment of the political aspect of the problem. Perhaps surprisingly, the "Common Statement" contains no joint reinterpretation of the Lutheran Confessions and *Pastor Aeternus*, nor any argument for their compatibility at the level of doctrinal or systematic ecclesiology. There are brief overtures in that direction in the independent "Reflections" of the Lutheran and Roman Catholic participants,[23] but in the "Common Statement" the approach is different. The response to this issue is contained in a section entitled, "Toward the Renewal of Papal Structures," which is essentially a call for *institutional* changes in the present exercise of papal primacy for the sake of unity.

The report wisely does not spell out the necessary changes in detail but sets forth three "Norms for Renewal" as guidance: the "principle of legitimate diversity," the "principle of collegiality," and the "principle of subsidiarity."[24] Much could and should be said about the deeper theological grounds for these principles and their appropriate application to the life of the church. I want to suggest, though, that what is at stake is the political credibility of the papal primacy as an institution in service to the mission of the whole church. In both East and West, justly or unjustly, there is a deeply engrained and widely distributed perception that the papacy stands for the precise opposites of the principles listed above: for the uniform imposition of the customs and outlook of the Roman Church on other churches, for an exclusive arrogation of significant authority and leadership to itself, and for the top-down micromanagement of ecclesial life in such a way that no decisions of importance may be made anywhere but in Rome. What the report is implying, I believe, is that no restatement

22. In the present situation, I think it needs to be said that we cannot assume that widespread Protestant admiration for the pope as man and Christian witness translates into a positive attitude toward the papacy as an institution and an order of church governance.

23. Cf. *PPUC*, pp. 27-28, 34-36.

24. *PPUC*, pp. 19-20.

of the theological rationale for papal primacy will suffice by itself to overcome this; what is called for is decisive action by which the papacy would identify itself in unmistakable ways, in practice and at the level of structures, with the affirmation of legitimate diversity, the collegial exercise of authority, and the wide diffusion of responsibility within the church. Only then will it be possible for its service of love, in the words of Pope John Paul II, to be "recognized" as such "by all concerned."[25]

Twenty-five years later, we can only marvel at the confidence with which the dialogue marched into what has turned out to be a dense thicket of difficulties. Thus the Roman Catholic participants wrote, with what now seems poignant naivete, that "one may foresee that voluntary limitations by the pope of the exercise of his jurisdiction will accompany the growing vitality of the organs of collegial government, so that checks and balances in the supreme power may be effectively recognized."[26] So far, at least, things have turned out differently, and it is not difficult to identify the unforeseen factor which has frustrated this good-hearted prophecy: there is no structural reform that the papacy could undertake in order to make its ministry more credible ecumenically that would not immediately become entangled in the internal politics of the Roman Catholic Church and be perceived as a victory for the "liberal" side in the ongoing internal Catholic conflict.

The ironies here are considerable. The suspicion sometimes entertained by conservatives in the Roman Catholic Church, that non-Catholic ecumenists and Catholic liberals are allied in a conspiracy to undermine papal authority, is almost completely groundless. Non–Roman Catholic ecumenists who propose structural reforms of the papacy are most likely to be orthodox moderates with a keen sense of the centrifugal forces threatening their own communions, and a high appreciation of the role an ecumenically renewed papacy could play in strengthening the pull of the apostolic center in all the churches.[27] What is proposed in one political context as an affirmation of the papacy, a way of extending the ecumenical reach of its ministry, is perceived as subversion of the papacy in the alternative political context of Catholic internal strife.

---

25. *Ut Unum Sint,* No. 95.

26. *PPUC,* p. 21.

27. Cf., for a recent Lutheran example, Carl E. Braaten, *Mother Church: Ecclesiology and Ecumenism* (Minneapolis: Augsburg Fortress, 1998).

We find ourselves, with these observations, standing once again before the horizon of mission, for the real question at stake here is the role of the papacy within the mission of the universal church. For nearly two centuries, since the papacy of Gregory XVI, but in continuity with its history throughout this millennium, the Roman see has pursued a clear conception of its mission: to exercise a close and watchful discipline over the churches in its care in order to protect the faithful from the disintegrative acids of modernity. Some popes have aspired to do more and other things, but this has been the constant baseline. I do not believe that we should underestimate either the costs or the achievements of this policy. The modern papacy has a grandeur to which neither the carping of its critics nor the sometimes insipid apologies of its defenders does full justice. But however we evaluate the papal strategy of the last two centuries, one thing is undeniable: it is a pre-ecumenical strategy. That is, it was formulated at a time when it was plausible to assume that the pope could fulfill his mission as universal pastor through a pastoral relationship to the Roman Catholic Church alone.

This is, to be sure, an easy assumption even today. Though the Reformation left the pope with only portions of the Latin patriarchate, the Latin patriarchate has for its part expanded, through the movements of peoples and the labors of missionaries, to extend over most of the globe. Pastoral care of a billion Christians will doubtless keep any pope occupied with a sufficiency of useful and absorbing day-to-day tasks. The Roman Catholic Church is big enough and complex enough to function as a world of its own.

Nevertheless, the situation has changed theologically; new perceptions have come on the scene. The recognition at Vatican II that baptized Christians separated from Rome are nonetheless "in a certain communion with the Catholic Church even though this communion is imperfect,"[28] would seem to imply that such Christians, along with the churches and ecclesial communities in which they find access to salvation, are proper objects of the pope's pastoral concern, even though this relationship cannot presently be perfected. It is not so easy now to say that the pope can be universal pastor simply by virtue of the discipline exercised from Rome over the Roman Catholic communion. Moreover, it might now seem worrisome that the institutional form of that discipline, however effective in

28. *Redintegratio Unitatis,* No. 4.

111

its own sphere, creates thorny barriers between the Petrine ministry and great multitudes of the sheep entrusted to its care. Thus we see, most eloquently in *Ut Unum Sint* but also in other expressions of the recent popes, the stirrings of vocational restlessness, a concern to find a way to feed those other sheep, to hearken to the Lord's call to strengthen and sustain those other brethren.

Such beginnings are to be treasured and cultivated, but we should not be surprised if they are a long time coming to fruition. Though it is clear that Catholic dogma does not unalterably mandate the present centralized structures,[29] they have behind them the momentum of a millennium of papal history, as well as the powerful dynamics of the strife within the Roman Catholic Church to which reference has been made. Indeed, the concrete pastoral tasks with which the popes are confronted in the Latin Church, the immediate struggles and opportunities that arise within the present Roman Catholic order of things, will doubtless always tend to take priority over merely notional and uncertain ecumenical possibilities.

This raises a question to which we must return at the end of this essay: do the ecumenical possibilities have to remain merely notional, or are there ways in which the papacy could enter into real though imperfect pastoral relationships with separated churches and ecclesial communities, this side of full communion? First, however, we must turn to the second document of the U.S. Lutheran-Catholic dialogue to address the papacy, and therewith to the problem of teaching authority.

The Problem of Teaching Authority

The 1978 report of the U.S. dialogue, entitled "Teaching Authority and Infallibility in the Church," has awakened fewer resonances in the life of the churches than the 1974 report on papal primacy. This is so in part, I fear, because this report is simply less successful than its predecessor. While it contains any number of insightful observations, as well as important tactical recommendations to which we shall return, it does not achieve a strategic perspective on the issues comparable to that of the earlier report. This

---

29. Cf. J. M. R. Tillard, *The Bishop of Rome* (London: SPCK; Wilmington, Del.: M. Glazier, 1983), and more recently, Hermann J. Pottmeyer, *Towards a Papacy in Communion: Perspectives from Vatican Councils I and II* (New York: Crossroad, 1998).

is partly due, I suspect, to the circumstances of the times. This round of the U.S. dialogue took place during the years when the Hans Küng affair was approaching its climax, and the dialogue was to some degree distracted by Küng's attempt to turn modern historical consciousness into a weapon against the very idea of infallible — or more precisely, irreformable — teaching. In this way, I believe, the dialogue was drawn into premature focus on *infallibility* and paid far too little attention to the underlying problem of teaching authority as such.[30]

The truth is that, despite its inflammatory sound, papal infallibility has turned out to be something of a red herring in the ecumenical discussion. The Catholic Church does not turn out, upon examination, to be claiming any of the preposterous things that the term tends to suggest; it seems that in the end no more is involved than the combination of primacy and magisterium. Thus a theologian so disinclined to revisionism on this point as Hans Urs von Balthasar was ready to grant that the term "infallibility" might obscure more than it clarified, and did not balk at Hans Frei's suggestion that the real issue might be more clearly indicated by speaking of the *Letztverbindlichkeit* under certain conditions of papal acts defining faith and morals.[31] That is to say, when the bishop of Rome bears witness to the apostolic tradition *ex cathedra,* in his capacity as universal pastor, his testimony has a binding force that is final, and admits no appeal; and it can be relied on, by virtue of Christ's promises to the whole church, not necessarily to be wise or well-stated or beyond improvement, but nevertheless to represent the faith revealed to Peter, not by flesh and blood but by the Father in heaven. The content of the infallibility claim is thus twofold: first, that the pope as universal pastor has legitimate authority under certain conditions to bring to a definitive end conflict and uncertainty regarding faith and morals, and second, that there are grounds for confidence that in this role the pope will not alienate the church from the apostolic faith. Thus the meaning of infallibility turns out to be entirely dependent on the way in which primacy and teaching authority are understood and practiced.

30. The "Lutheran Reflections" (*TAIC,* pp. 59-68) in particular focus almost exclusively on "Lutheran problems with traditional infallibility claims and language" (60) and fail to bring into the dialogue the wider discussion of teaching authority in the Reformation and the subsequent Lutheran tradition. This leaves hanging in the air the very interesting practical suggestions with which the "Lutheran Reflections" close, since these have to do more broadly with *magisterium,* rather than narrowly with infallibility.
31. Hans Urs von Balthasar, *Der antirömische Affekt* (Freiburg: Herder, 1974), p. 184.

It would seem clear then that ecumenical progress requires prior discussion of the very idea of a teaching office with binding authority; we must, so to speak, come to terms with *Verbindlichkeit* before we can profitably address the problem of *Letztverbindlichkeit.* The crucial ecumenical issue is not the philosophical hermeneutics of infallibility but the essentially ecclesial-political problem of authority. To make the point concretely: so long as Lutherans boggle at the teaching of the Augsburg Confession that it belongs to the office of a bishop *by divine right* "to judge doctrine and to condemn doctrine that is contrary to the gospel,"[32] no really fruitful discussion will be possible of the claim of the Roman bishop to judge doctrine definitively as universal pastor.

The Lutheran Reformation's concern with this theme focused on what we would now call the relationship of the teaching office to the whole body of the faithful. Starting from scriptural affirmations of the priestly dignity of the whole people of God, the Reformers were critical of accounts of magisterium that seemed to suggest a one-sided dependence of the faithful on the teaching office, a clerical monopoly on the true knowledge of Christ. The apostles have delivered the holy gospel to the whole church, and *all* the faithful take part in various ways in the transmission of the apostolic tradition from age to age. The special vocation of the ministerial office to teach and judge doctrine, which the Reformers by no means denied, must be located *within* this communion of knowledge and responsibility. Practically this means that the judgments of the teaching office cannot claim purely formal or a priori validity but must appeal for recognition by the faithful on the basis of shared standards of legitimacy, in particular Holy Scripture. As Martin Chemnitz, the great Lutheran theologian of the second generation, put it: ". . . the interpreter must show the reasons and bases of his interpretation so clearly and certainly that also others who themselves do not have the gift of interpretation may be able to understand and grasp them."[33] The judgment of the teaching office seeks by its intelligible appeal to Scripture to elicit the "Amen" of the people of God and thus be confirmed as the judgment of the whole church.

It is just possible today that agreement could be reached between this Reformation perspective and the teaching of the Roman Catholic Church.

32. *Augsburg Confession,* Article 28.
33. Martin Chemnitz, *Examination of the Council of Trent,* vol. 1, trans. Fred Kramer (St. Louis: Concordia, 1971), p. 216.

It is striking, for example, how *Dei Verbum,* the Constitution on Divine Revelation of Vatican II, locates the magisterial task of "authentically interpreting the word of God" within the shared reception of the apostolic tradition by pastors and people together: "Clinging to this, the entire holy people, in union with its pastors, perseveres continually in the teaching and communion of the apostles, the breaking of bread, and the prayers (Acts 2:42), so that in the holding, practicing, and professing of the faith that has been handed down there is a singular unanimity *(singularis conspiratio)* of the bishops and the faithful together."[34] The magisterium of the pastors, so located, "is not above the word of God" thus jointly received, "but ministers to it, teaching nothing but what has been handed down, insofar as, by the divine command and with the help of the Holy Spirit, it hears that word devotedly, safeguards it reverently, and expounds it faithfully, and draws everything which it sets forth to be believed as divinely revealed from this one deposit of the faith."[35]

The agreement with the Reformation would be quite substantial if Lutherans and Catholics could go on to say together, as the U.S. dialogue report believed possible, "that in the Church universal the harmony between the teaching of the Ministers and its acceptance by the faithful constitutes a sign of the fidelity of that teaching to the gospel. . . ."[36] This is not a call for procedural democracy, with official teaching subject to vote or some other form of immediate ratification. It is a recognition of spiritual reciprocity, the mutual dependence of pastors and people within their common reception and discernment of the apostolic faith. Vatican II seems at various points strongly to suggest such reciprocity without ever quite affirming it undeniably. Yet it seems clear today that the Roman Catholic Church is by no means committed to an account of teaching authority as, in Chemnitz's phrase, "dictatorial power," exempt from any obligation to make credible appeal to shared norms and to seek the "Amen" of the faithful on that basis.

These hopeful possibilities have been widely and profitably discussed in the ecumenical literature,[37] but here too we must temper our hopeful-

---

34. *Dei Verbum,* No. 10.

35. *Dei Verbum,* No. 10.

36. *TAIC,* p. 31.

37. Cf. recently Wolfhart Pannenberg, "A Lutheran's Reflections on the Petrine Ministry of the Bishop of Rome," *Communio* 25 (Winter 1988): 604-618; on this point see esp. pp. 616-618.

ness with the recollection that we are seeking the reconciliation not of theologies but of churches, actual communities in the untidiness of history. To reconcile Chemnitz and Vatican II would be a wonderful thing, but it would not yet be the reconciliation of the Lutheran and Roman Catholic churches. Each of our communions stands in a complex historical relationship to the normative traditions named "Vatican II" and "the Reformation." Within the Roman Catholic Church it is, to say the least, controversial what implications the nuances and insights of the Vatican II documents might properly have for the way in which magisterium has come to be exercised over the past several centuries. The Lutheran churches today are separated from the Reformation by nearly five hundred years of eventful history, through which the notions of authority and freedom have hardly come unscathed. Much could be said about the difficulties thus generated on both sides, but it seems appropriate to focus here on the Lutherans.

The Reformers envisioned a vigorous practice of magisterium in the churches, led by the chief pastors and parish clergy, but appealing to the discernment of a people formed by Scripture and catechism and issuing in firm and binding corporate judgments. Such a practice of magisterium was highly necessary, the Reformers believed, because the devil never ceases to attack the apostolic gospel, attempting by open or covert means to deprive the church of the true knowledge of Christ. But when we look at the mainline Lutheranism of the Northern Hemisphere today, at the European *Volkskirchen* and the large Lutheran denominations of North America, it is clear not only that no such corporate discernment is presently practiced, but also that such practice has become fundamentally unimaginable. It may be that in some parts of the Southern Hemisphere, the emerging Lutheran churches could yet develop rather differently, but in Lutheranism's historic northern bastions, magisterium as envisioned by the Reformers would now be regarded as no less oppressive than the magisterium of the bishop of Rome.

There are doubtless many causes of this development. I have written elsewhere of the role which modern notions of freedom have played in the disappearance of church discipline within the Protestant mainline.[38] But

38. Cf. David S. Yeago, "The Office of the Keys: On the Disappearance of Discipline in Protestant Modernity," in Braaten and Jenson, eds., *Marks of the Body of Christ* (Grand Rapids: Eerdmans, 1999).

on this occasion I would like to focus on something simpler, yet perhaps more fundamental. Despite what I have suggested is a certain strategic weakness in the 1978 Report, the Lutheran participants identified quite correctly the horizon of concern within which the issue of teaching authority becomes inescapable:

> We share the conviction that decisions about the truth of the gospel have to be made for the sake of the gospel's life in the world. Consequently, we affirm a Ministry which has the responsibility of reformulating doctrine in fidelity to the Scripture when circumstances require.[39]

Note that here once again we are brought to the horizon of mission. The urgency of magisterium becomes clear only in the light of a particular account of the mission of the church, of the ends of its existence in history. The church is understood as a community of witness, entrusted with a word of determinate content, the word of the gospel. This gospel is not easily received by a world with deep investments in pride, fear, and violence, so that, in Luther's words, "it is the most unvarying fate of the word of God to have the world in a state of tumult because of it."[40] This gospel is thus a message with enemies,[41] and the church is constantly exposed to temptation, tribulation, and seduction from within and without, aimed at blurring the edges and distorting the outline of the message entrusted to it. Thus it is possible to say that "decisions about the truth of the gospel have to be made for the sake of the gospel's life in the world." But in the mainline Lutheran churches of the Northern Hemisphere today, it is not at all clear that such decisions "have to be made," and in fact, in most such churches, there are no longer any provisions for making them.[42] Far from being recognized as a normal exigency of the church's mission, moreover, doctrinal debate and discernment are regularly objected to as a distraction from mission.

39. *TAIC,* pp. 66-67.
40. Martin Luther, *The Bondage of the Will,* Luther's Works, vol. 33 (Philadelphia: Fortress Press, 1972), p. 52.
41. Cf. Stanley Hauerwas, "Preaching as though We Had Enemies," *First Things 53* (May 1995): 45-49.
42. For a sketch of a church order designed to promote *magisterium* as understood by the Reformers, cf. Robert W. Jenson, "Sovereignty in the Church," in Carl E. Braaten, ed., *The New Church Debate: Issues Facing American Lutheranism* (Philadelphia: Fortress, 1983), pp. 39-53. This essay was "the voice of one crying in the wilderness," but should not be allowed to be forgotten.

Clearly there are different conceptions of the church's mission at work here; the understanding of mission that informs the present life of the mainline Lutheran churches is not that evoked by the dialogue report. While the rhetoric of witness and testimony still has a strong surface appeal in the churches descended from the Reformation, their real working sense of mission is far more deeply shaped, I believe, by centuries of state church life in Europe, and by the North American Lutheran struggle to incorporate the influx of German and Scandinavian immigrants in the late nineteenth and early twentieth centuries. In other words, mainline Lutheran churches in Europe and North America typically conceive of themselves not as heralds of the gospel but as providers of the consolations of religion to extensive populations. Within such a sense of mission, magisterium looks very different than it does in an ecclesiology of witness. The first obligation of the church as a service provider is not to speak a particular truth with clarity, but to remain available to the population it is called to serve. Magisterium, whether on the Reformation or the Roman model, seems to hamper that availability, and so to deprive the people of the consolations to which they have a right.

How did this happen to the Lutherans, with their history of doctrinal passion? The causes are surely complex, but let me point to one contributing factor. It was, I believe, an unintended consequence of nineteenth-century confessionalism that doctrinal questions came to be formulated not as questions of truth but as questions of identity; the central issue imperceptibly came to be not the *evangelica veritas,* the gospel truth that so exercised the Reformers, but "our identity as Lutherans," a concept which the Reformers would have found difficult to comprehend. Thus doctrine has come to be seen as part of an inherited ethnicity to which the church is tempted to cling when it is challenged to reach out instead to new or changed constituents. Indeed, so complete has been the identification of Lutheranism with a quasi-ethnic "identity" that those who want to reach out evangelistically beyond the Nordic and Germanic tribes often take it for granted that in order to do so they must suppress the label "Lutheran." Much more could be said about this; it would also be possible to ask whether a parallel set of factors may have shaped the development of magisterial practice in the modern Roman Catholic Church. But enough has been said, perhaps, to provide a further illustration of a main thesis of this paper: the reconciliation of the churches will require not only advances in theological insight but also profound changes in their lived and practiced sense of mission.

With particular reference to the Lutheran churches let me say clearly: as long as we proceed on our current deep assumptions about our mission, about the ends of our existence, there will be no real prospect of our reconciliation with a Petrine ministry that takes the task of magisterium seriously. A Lutheran church in which a Reformation account of teaching authority was translated into living practice could undoubtedly engage in a lively exchange with Rome, with the prospect of learning and growth on both sides, leading very likely to eventual convergence. But that will only happen if Lutheran churches reorder their corporate lives to pursue very different ends from those which now draw them.

There are small but significant reasons for hope that this may actually begin to occur, at least in North America, in the decades to come. The decadence of our present orientation is increasingly obvious, and a quiet consensus seems to be taking form in significant quarters of the Protestant mainline that survival with integrity requires the gradual reorganization of our congregations as culturally independent communities of intentional witness, proclaiming alike by their teaching and their life together the reconciliation of the world to God in Jesus Christ.[43] Such moves must of course reckon with a countervailing momentum built up over centuries of Protestant history. Nothing is guaranteed. But it is at least clear that such communities of intentional witness would have to confront the question of magisterium in new ways; they would need once again the capacity to make corporately binding "decisions about the truth of the gospel" precisely "for the sake of the life of the gospel in the world."

For our purposes here, what I hope to convey is a sense of how deep the ecumenical question, and particularly the matter of the papacy, bites into the present lives of all our churches. Our disunity cannot be neatly separated from the whole range of deformations in mission and life that they have suffered as they have lurched through the history of this past millennium, nor can reconciliation be conceived as a mere external coor-

43. Especially important is the work of the Gospel and Our Culture Network; cf. the programmatic volume edited by Darrell L. Guder, *Missional Church: A Vision for the Sending of the Church in North America* (Grand Rapids: Eerdmans, 1998). Though the ecclesiology of this book is not all that the Lutheran–Roman Catholic dialogue might require, it nonetheless represents a prospect of considerable ecumenical importance. I am grateful to my colleague Phil Baker for drawing my attention to this body of thought.

dination of estranged communities, uninvolved with any transformation of what they inwardly are.

"Magisterial Mutuality" — A Way Forward?

To this point our reflections have taken a path that might be described as severe if not discouraging. The ecumenical problem of the papacy cannot be resolved, I have argued, apart from far-reaching changes in the ethos and practice of all our churches, changes which none of us has the wisdom to define precisely or the power to bring about. There is no evading the astringency of these conclusions, and it will do us no harm if we leave this conference with a renewed awareness that the future is in God's hands and not in our own. Nevertheless, that awareness, when it is authentic, is never paralyzing but frees us to undertake in faith the small steps that are our duty here and now.

In that spirit, I want to conclude by asking what present possibilities there might be for giving greater embodiment to the real though imperfect communion in which, by common consensus, the Lutheran and Roman Catholic churches now stand. Is there anything hopeful to be done this side of full communion, and likewise this side of the great changes that I believe will be necessary in the end? I will speak about Lutherans and Roman Catholics, though what I shall propose might well be of wider application.

In the first place, we could and should give greater symbolic weight and formality to our communion in prayer. My denomination could undertake to pray quite specifically for the bishop of Rome at all its assemblies, national or synodical. Such prayer would not involve acceptance of Roman primacy as defined at Vatican I, but it should be explicitly understood as public recognition of the pope's leading role in the world Christian community, and an acknowledgment that we too have a stake in the health of the papacy. Likewise, my denomination could formally communicate the names of all our ministers of oversight to Rome on the occasion of their election, with a request that prayer be offered on their behalf in the worship of the Roman Church. For Rome to accede to this request, which would adapt a sign of mutuality from the ancient church, would not settle the question of the authenticity of ministries, which is still unresolved between us, but it would constitute an acknowledgment that Lutheran bishops are (or should be) engaged in ecclesially significant tasks, however defined, and that Rome too has a stake in their integrity and effectiveness. Such formal commitments to mutual prayer would not exclude but should include similar commitments between Lutheran and Roman Catholic churches in particular regions and localities. In all such cases, the existing bond of communion would receive public recognition, and to that extent be affirmed and strengthened. Furthermore, we should not discount the possibility that God in his unfathomable mercy might actually respond to our prayers, the consequences of which would be incalculable.

My second suggestion presses a bit harder at the limits of the presently possible. One of the most valuable features of the 1978 report on teaching authority is its introduction of the notion of "magisterial mutuality" as an intermediate form of ecumenical reconciliation. Precisely in order to do justice to the existing real communion between Lutheran and Roman Catholic churches, the report called for the development of structures of mutual consultation and colloquy in matters of teaching and discernment. The Lutheran participants made the following recommendations, among others, to the Lutheran churches:

> . . . that they facilitate Catholic contributions to the process of formulating Lutheran positions on doctrinal and ethical issues. . . . that they develop structures for regular consultation with Catholic bishops on the local and national levels regarding matters of mutual concern. . . . that they declare their willingness to participate in a worldwide and ecumenically-based magisterium; this participation might take many forms. . . .[44]

I would like to renew these recommendations, which have not been received or even seriously discussed in the Lutheran churches, and at the same time add another, in the same spirit but more directly focused on the relationship between Lutherans and the Petrine ministry of the bishop of Rome. While I have suggested that the authentic practice of magisterium, as envisioned by the Reformers, has become rather alien to us, there are nonetheless occasions on which denominations like mine appoint commissions, boards, and panels to consider questions of faith and morals. Nothing would stop us from making it a regular practice on such occasions to request formally the advice and counsel of the Holy See. This would imply no *a priori* commitment to follow Rome's counsel. But it

44. *TAIC,* p. 68.

should include an undertaking always to respond in detail and in writing to whatever is received from Rome, and to make the correspondence public unless unusual considerations intervene. Such a policy would by no means constitute recognition of papal jurisdiction as defined at Vatican I, but it would be an acknowledgment of the significance for the whole church of the papacy's witness to the apostolic faith. It would be a recognition that though we may not always follow that witness, we should nonetheless never ignore it.

Such an arrangement would be promising in various ways for both churches. It would allow the papacy to enter into real though imperfect pastoral relationships with the "other sheep" from which it has been estranged, and explore unfamiliar modes of pastoral communication without threatening its pastoral and disciplinary grip on the Roman Catholic Church. A papal magisterium with valued and long-standing relationships in which it had become accustomed to proceed by persuasion rather than command might over time find new departures imaginable. On the Lutheran side, the self-imposed obligation to listen and respond to the counsel of the papacy could help free our deliberations from their frequent North American parochialism and give a considerable boost to their doctrinal seriousness and credibility. While this arrangement would not constitute full communion, such an "imperfect" relationship would be capable of growth in unpredictable ways and directions. It is worth remembering that in the first millennium, before the Great Schism, and still in the West for many centuries thereafter, the papacy related to the different local churches in a great variety of contingent, historically developed ways; the concrete relations of the pope to the communion of the churches were not constructed according to any plan but grew in the freedom of the Spirit. And so, we may hope, it could be again.

To be sure, I can well imagine the wall of hesitancy and resistance that might well arise before such a proposal. The Holy See would worry, no doubt, about appearing to compromise its claims, and I can only imagine what the *Lutheran Commentator* would say. Some Roman Catholic progressives would be angry, as some were angry at *Ut Unum Sint,* at Rome appearing more ready to reach out to Protestants than to dissident Catholics. Those with revisionist agendas in the ELCA might see such an arrangement as damaging to their prospects.

Nevertheless, the proposal itself does not seem to me intrinsically extreme or unworkable — it might even be a reasonable next step in the wake of our achievement of fundamental consensus on the doctrine of justification. How better for Lutherans to affirm concretely that we no longer regard the pope as an outright enemy of the *evangelica veritas*? Luther was willing to kiss the pope's feet if he would allow the pure preaching of the gospel. Now that we agree that he does allow it, why should we not be willing on significant occasions to ask his advice and listen to his counsel?

The Problem of Authority
in Evangelical Christianity

RICHARD J. MOUW

What can an evangelical contribute to a discussion of "Church Unity and the Papal Office" in a context where the other conversation partners represent Roman Catholicism, Orthodoxy, Anglicanism, Lutheranism and conciliar Protestantism? Anyone who is at all familiar with the so-called "conservative evangelical" movement in North America knows that we are not very fond of the papal office. Nor do we hold to the kinds of ecclesiological views that fit easily within the categories that are taken for granted by the other traditions represented in this consultation.

To put it in personal terms: when I listen to discussions among Christians who are concerned about the papacy and related matters, I feel like someone attending a family gathering after having lived for a long time away from home. My relatives are discussing matters of disagreement that I know little about, yet I listen with more than detached interest. I don't know exactly how to enter into the arguments, but neither can I convince myself that the discussions are none of my business.

Why *do* evangelicals have a difficult time participating in conversations of this sort? Why is it that we are not sure where we can even find our entry points into the kind of framework that the pope lays out in his encyclical about unity? As I read *Ut Unum Sint*, I looked without success for some overt signals that Pope John Paul II meant to find a place for us in his quest for Christian unity. The fact is that we evangelicals do need some reassurance in this regard. This pope has a habit of making rather frequent negative references to "sects," as in his "Opening Address to the Fourth General Conference of the Latin American Episcopate," where he issued a lengthy warning against those "rapacious wolves" who lead various divisive "sects and 'pseudospiritual' movements,"[1] a warning that he repeated in this year's "Ecclesia in America."[2]

To be sure, the pope never explicitly links evangelicals with these sectarian movements. But certainly many Catholics who take the pope's warnings to heart do see the links in this way. For example, in the 1994 volume, *Sects and New Religious Movements: An Anthology of Texts from the Catholic Church 1986-1994*, published by the Vatican, the term "sect" is explained by Cardinal Ernesto Corripio Ahumada:

> The Christian sects are the most numerous: the majority are Pentecostals; there are Baptists, Adventists and independent denominations. Almost all these groups call themselves "evangelical churches." The most widespread pseudo-Christian sects are the Jehovah's Witnesses and the Mormons.[3]

I really do not want to be detained here, however, by issues of rhetoric — especially since we evangelicals are not exactly models of rhetorical politeness. Furthermore, these kinds of characterizations are not indicative of the whole scenario in relations between Catholics and evangelicals. In recent years some promising new efforts at better understanding have been initiated on several fronts — especially in the Vatican-Pentecostal dialogue, as well as in the "Evangelicals and Catholics Together" project. I welcome the opportunity to make yet another attempt at clarifying some key issues here, even if I have to move rather quickly over some important theological territory in doing so.

Strictly speaking, of course, "evangelical" simply denotes a commitment to the Christian gospel. In that sense all Christian believers are evangelicals. But I will be using it as a label that has come in North America to refer to a rather loose trans-denominational coalition of groups and min-

1. John Paul II, "Opening Address to the Fourth General Conference of Latin American Episcopate," *Origins* 22:19 (Oct. 22, 1992): 321-332.

2. John Paul II, "Ecclesia in America," *Origins* 28:33 (Feb. 4, 1999): 589.

3. *Sects and New Religious Movements: An Anthology of Texts from the Catholic Church 1986-1994*, edited by The Working Group on New Religious Movements (Washington, D.C.: United States Catholic Conference, Inc., 1995), p. 4.

istries that have their origins in various branches of Protestant pietism and pietist-type groups.

Pietism is a pattern of Christianity that has emphasized the experiential dimensions of the Christian faith. European pietism had its beginnings in a reaction against a highly intellectualized orthodoxy that had come to characterize many Lutheran and Reformed churches in the century or so after the Reformation. Early pietist groups protested what they saw as an elevation — to use a favorite pietist labeling scheme — of "head knowledge" over "heart knowledge."

This pietist concern for curbing rationalist tendencies took on a new urgency in the eighteenth and nineteenth centuries, when Enlightenment thought made serious inroads into Christian community. This time the battle was not against a dead orthodoxy, but with a live heterodoxy that saw enlightened human reason as the highest standard of truth in the universe. Today's evangelical movement includes groups whose histories can be directly traced back to these reactions, as well as to other groups — Wesleyans, Pentecostals, sectarian "primitivists," and others — who emphasize similar experiential motifs. We present-day evangelicals, like the pietists of the past, stress the need for a religion of "the heart." We want individuals to experience the regeneration of the inner self, so that the claims of the gospel are appropriated in a very personal way. And we take seriously the obligation to evangelize people of no faith, of other faiths, and of "nominal" Christian faith. To be sure, we also pay close attention to doctrinal formulations. We care about the way people speak theologically about the authority of Scripture, the virgin birth, the atoning work of Christ, and the like. If the Christian faith rests in a fundamental way on a heartfelt trust in a Savior, then how we understand the person and work of that Savior — and the authority of the Book that instructs us regarding his redemptive program — is a matter of profound importance.

In the brief account that I have just given of the pietist and pietist-type character of evangelicalism, I have made much of the sorts of things that evangelicals emphasize — and indeed on the kinds of things that we emphasize *in reaction* to things that bother us about the ways in which other people spell out their understandings of the nature of Christianity. This is intentional on my part. Evangelicalism is a protest movement. To list what evangelicals, qua evangelicals, believe is to record a set of emphases that are meant as spiritual and theological correctives. For example, even though many of us in the evangelical camp have long ago ceased to think of ourselves as "fundamentalists," we still want to go out of our way to make it clear that we share the theological concerns that the fundamentalists earlier in this century defended against the emerging modernist movement. We want to emphasize the importance of a faith system in which beliefs like the virgin birth of Jesus, his full divinity, the blood sacrifice character of his atoning work, the blessed hope of his second coming — where beliefs of this sort are clearly and unambiguously confessed.

It is not uncommon for other Christians — say, Roman Catholics or Lutherans or Eastern Orthodox believers — to point out that this does not amount to a robust theological perspective. Why is it that our evangelical list of "fundamentals" makes no mention, for example, of anything ecclesiological, or of the sacraments? The honest response is that of course the list of things that evangelicals typically emphasize does not come close to comprising a comprehensive theological perspective when compared to classical confessional traditions. And it is regrettable that large numbers of evangelicals do in fact operate with an extremely limited theological perspective. But not all of us do so. For some of us "evangelical" is best thought of as a theological modifier rather than as a noun. We do not think that label can stand alone when sorting out theological systems.

For example, in order to provide an accurate identification of my own theological position I find it necessary to say that I am an "evangelical Calvinist." I take the "Calvinist" part of this very seriously. In addition to endorsing the soteriology set forth by John Calvin in his *Institutes of the Christian Religion* and developed further in the confessions and catechisms of the sixteenth and seventeenth centuries, I also adhere to the ecclesiology and sacramentalism of the Reformed tradition. I judge that this provides me with a fairly robust theological perspective, one that leads me into interesting arguments with persons who use the term "evangelical" to modify other theological perspectives.

But the "evangelical" modifier itself is also important to my understanding of my theological identity. It means, for one thing, that as a good pietist I will worry about certain kinds of scholastic tendencies in some branches of Reformed orthodoxy. And it also means that I will be inclined to warn against both modernist and post-modernist revisionisms in the mainline Presbyterian denomination to which I belong. And it means that, while I enjoy arguing points of theology with those who attach the "evangelical" label to other confessional perspectives, I also see myself as being

127

in common cause with them in promoting trans-denominational programs of spiritual and theological renewal.

Back in my graduate school days, when I was struggling to clarify for myself where I belonged on the existing spectrum of spiritual-theological identities, I read James Packer's little book *"Fundamentalism" and the Word of God*. Packer's way of sorting out the issues was immensely helpful to me, and had a permanent impact on my thinking about the basic issues. Packer made his case for the evangelical perspective by outlining, first of all, what he took to be "the common ground" on which all Christians stand. We all believe, he said, that Christianity is a revealed religion, and that authority in the Christian community

> derives from this revelation. . . . It is God speaking in Christ, and God's word spoken through Christ that is ultimately authoritative; it is the Bible that bears authoritative witness to the speaking of that word; and it is the Holy Spirit who, in every age, mediates that authoritative word to the individual Christian and the Church.[4]

Again, that is what Packer took to be the Christian consensus. The disagreements arise, he observed, when we ask more specific questions of this sort:

> How should we set about discovering just what this word of God is? By what channel exactly is it mediated from the past to the present? From what source may we gain authoritative guidance as to what God has and has not authoritatively said? When Christian opinions differ, where should be the final court of appeal? This is the problem of authority.[5]

Packer went on to examine at length three different ways of answering these questions. For evangelicals, the final court of appeal is to be found in "Scripture as interpreted by itself"; "Romanists, some Anglo-Catholics and Orthodox" locate it in "Scripture as interpreted (and in some measure amplified) by official ecclesiastical sources"; and "Liberal Protestants" look to "Scripture as evaluated in terms of extra-biblical principles by individual Christian[s]."[6] While these characterizations are obviously not fully

4. J. I. Packer, *"Fundamentalism" and the Word of God: Some Evangelical Principles* (Grand Rapids: Wm. B. Eerdmans Publishing Co., 1958), p. 46.

5. Packer, *"Fundamentalism,"* p. 46.

6. Packer, *"Fundamentalism,"* pp. 46-47.

adequate as accounts of how to sort out the various perspectives on authority that are at work in the Christian community, they helped me at an important stage in my theological journey to focus on some basic choices I had to make in my own thinking, and Packer's way of stating the positive case for evangelicalism has had a long-term influence on my theological development.

In spite of the impression sometimes given by typologies of the sort that Packer sets forth, evangelicals have always had more affinity with Catholic views of authority than with the perspective of liberal Protestantism. The liberal reliance on "extra-biblical principles" was often motivated by a desire to reduce the scope of normative "supernatural" data; but our evangelical arguments with Roman Catholics have never been over that kind of reductionism. Indeed, if anything, we have found Catholics to be a little *too* inclined toward supernatural explanations. While, for example, we evangelicals have insisted in our arguments with liberals that it is important to believe in a literal virgin birth, Catholics have upped the supernaturalist ante by telling us that we also need to accept the dogma of Mary's assumption, body and soul, into the heavenly regions. We evangelicals passionately argue that real water miraculously changed into real wine at Cana of Galilee; but we can sound like religious skeptics when we respond to the Catholic insistence that real wine regularly turns into the real blood of Christ in the eucharistic celebration.

In our calmer moments, though, we evangelicals have actually celebrated our affinity with Catholicism on basic worldview issues. Here, for example, is how J. Gresham Machen put the matter in his 1923 book, *Christianity and Liberalism,* one of the classics of American evangelical thought:

> How great is the common heritage which unites the Roman Catholic Church, with its maintenance of the authority of Holy Scripture and with its acceptance of the great early creeds, to devout Protestants today! We would not indeed obscure the difference which divides us from Rome. The gulf is indeed profound. But profound as it is, it seems almost trifling compared to the abyss which stands between us and many ministers of our own Church.[7]

7. J. Gresham Machen, *Christianity and Liberalism* (Grand Rapids: Wm. B. Eerdmans Publishing Co., 1972), p. 52.

Machen is correct: we should be careful to pay close attention to the important difference between gulfs and abysses. He rightly sees our common fidelity to those teachings set forth in an authoritative Scripture as summarized in the early creeds as the basis for a significant bond between evangelicals and Roman Catholics. And while the many residual disagreements cannot be ignored, they are nonetheless of a different order than the arguments that we engage in with persons who reject key biblical teachings by appealing to the deliverances of the "enlightened" human spirit.

Evangelicals have similar reasons for welcoming the opportunities for dialogue with those post-liberal Protestants who have openly disassociated themselves from what they see as the regrettable influences of "the Enlightenment project" on much of mainline Protestantism during the past century. And in emphasizing the importance of the church as an authoritative communal interpreter of the biblical message, they have given evangelicals even more motivation for being clear about the differences between their own understanding of authority and those of Christians who strongly emphasize the normative character of the church's interpretive task.

These differences surfaced clearly in a casual exchange that I witnessed a while back, on the subject of homosexuality. Two clergy from the same mainline denomination, one of them an evangelical and the other a person influenced by post-liberal thinkers, were discussing their denominational debates on the topic, and they rather quickly signaled the fact that they both opposed the ordination of practicing homosexuals. As the conversation proceeded, however, they offered somewhat different ways of defending their opposition. The evangelical referred to the fact that the first chapter of Romans, as she interpreted it, clearly ruled out the legitimacy of any same-sex genital intimacy. The post-liberal replied that he also took the Romans 1 passage seriously, "since the church has traditionally chosen to treat this text as a source for normative guidance." The evangelical quickly responded that she would continue to take Romans 1 as authoritative even if the church decided *not* to treat it as normative. And the argument — a friendly one — proceeded from that point into a discussion of the proper locus of authority. During the course of that discussion the post-liberal made it clear that he did not think that the evangelical view gave adequate attention to the church's authoritative role as an interpretive community.

We evangelicals are often accused of having a weak ecclesiology.

Sometimes the truth of this accusation seems so obvious to the people who lodge it that no elaboration is deemed necessary. When an attempt is made to spell out what is meant, however, it usually has something to do with a lack of appreciation for corporate Christian existence, or even with a tendency toward an "anti-church" or an ecclesio-anarchistic posture, that is attributed to the evangelical movement.

There can be no arguing that the evangelical movement has very different attitudes toward denominational and conciliar structures than many other Christians. It is not altogether inaccurate, given the viewpoints with which evangelicalism is being compared, to say that evangelicals have a "weak" doctrine of the church. Whether this has to be seen as a defect, however, has much to do with the standards that we employ in diagnosing ecclesiological strengths and weaknesses. And our choice of standards will in turn have much to do with the way in which our theology of the church relates to other elements in our larger theological schemes.

The thrust of my own response to evangelicalism's critics on this point is formulated nicely by the Anglican evangelical Alister McGrath: "It is currently fashionable," he observes, "to speak of evangelicals as having an 'under-developed ecclesiology'; perhaps it might be suggested that it is others who have over-developed ecclesiologies?"[8] Let me state McGrath's point bluntly: in our efforts to evaluate critically "weak" doctrines of the church we ought not to be insensitive to the dangers posed by "strong" ecclesiologies. We evangelicals have long worried about ecclesiological perspectives that are so highly detailed and all consuming that they marginalize other important theological concerns. In a sense, this worry has its roots in the Reformation: when Luther raised a much-neglected soteriological concern about justification by faith, his critics regularly responded with complaints about his weak ecclesiology as allegedly evidenced in his lack of appreciation for the nuances of a proper account of churchly authority. This is but one of many examples of situations in which evangelical Protestants have experienced the heavy-handedness of a theological perspective that is dominated by ecclesiology.

Evangelicals approach ecclesiological discussions with clear memories of harsh voices from our collective past that sought to silence our pleas

8. Alister McGrath, "Evangelical Anglicanism: A Contradiction in Terms?" in R. T. France and A. E. McGrath, eds., *Evangelical Anglicans: Their Role and Influence in the Church Today* (London: SPCK, 1993), p. 14.

for renewal by calling us to "respect the structures," "follow due process," and "submit to the Body." If we evangelicals are suspicious of "strong" ecclesiologies, then, it is due at least in part to our experiences at the hands of those who have used ecclesiology as an instrument of control. Here is an instance where we may be more astute regarding the actual uses to which theology may be put than those of our critics who pride themselves on their "postmodern" sensitivities!

A central concern on the evangelical agenda, as I have already indicated, is the link between ecclesiology and soteriology. It is precisely because of this link that, in my experience at least, evangelicals and Roman Catholics often talk past each other in theological discussions. The most common pattern is one wherein evangelicals are thinking soteriologically — focusing on "salvation" questions — while Roman Catholics are thinking ecclesiologically — emphasizing the doctrine of the church.

This pattern came out poignantly at a meeting of a Roman Catholic and evangelical dialogue group in Los Angeles a few years ago. A Mexican-American Pentecostal pastor told of his experience of attending a Catholic funeral mass for a young man who had been killed in a gang-related incident. "The boy who died was a close friend of a young man in my church, so I went to the funeral. Dozens of gang members were there," he said. "I thought to myself, 'What a wonderful opportunity to talk to these young people about what it means to give their lives to Jesus Christ!' But the whole funeral was just business-as-usual. It took it for granted that everyone was a Christian, and there was no real explanation of what the gospel was all about!" A Mexican-American priest immediately responded to this complaint: "Business-as-usual is exactly what we *want* them to experience. We want to expose them to *church*. We want them to experience what it is like to deal with the issues of life and death in the normal context of the community of the faithful. Let them have a taste of what the 'ordinary' church is all about!"

This is a typical evangelical–Roman Catholic exchange. The evangelical wanted questions about how we are "saved" to be addressed explicitly; he wanted the unbelievers to be invited to accept the message of salvation as it is set forth in simple and direct terms. The Roman Catholic wanted to expose the unbelievers to the "normal" rituals of the churchly community, in the hope that the exposure itself — quite apart from an immediate conscious response to a gospel invitation — would be a means of grace.

After this initial exchange, though, the dialogue group worked to-

132

ward a more nuanced understanding on both sides. The Catholics admitted that it might be good to issue a call to discipleship in the situation described. The evangelicals conceded that the Holy Spirit can work in a covert manner, drawing sinners to Jesus by the less-than-fully-explicit communal witness of the Christian community as it gathers to do its "business as usual."

Real differences do remain, however. We evangelicals do give higher priority to "personal decision" questions and Roman Catholics to ecclesiological ones. But evangelicalism's long-standing suspicion of "over-developed" ecclesiologies should not be confused with ecclesiological indifference. While evangelicals like to insist that ecclesiological emphases should not be allowed to overwhelm other areas of theological focus, such as soteriology, Christology, and pneumatology, this does not mean that we are thereby guilty of de-emphasizing the importance of the doctrine of the church. We may be inclined, as McGrath puts it, toward a "minimalist ecclesiology";[9] but this should not be taken as a sign that we are less interested in ecclesiological questions than Christians who tend toward a more expansive ecclesiology. Indeed, a case can be made for the contention that an intentional minimalism in this area of theological concern can signal a deep commitment to a well-formed doctrine of the church. As Gillian Sumner — another Anglican evangelical — has put it, if evangelicals have placed a high value on "a well founded, scripturally based ecclesiology" that is nonetheless undeveloped in its treatment of ecclesiastical details, it is precisely because we have wanted to be open to the continuing reform of the church.[10]

Since the very notion of an intentional ecclesiological minimalism will not sit well with many other Christians, the perspective I am briefly describing here needs much more systematic amplification for the purposes of ecumenical consumption. I will not be able to provide that kind of detail here. But I do want to single out at least some features of evangelical ecclesiology for further clarification.

The first feature is one that I have just touched upon: the *fluid character* of evangelical ecclesiology. When I was a member of the Calvin College Department of Philosophy, we met every week as faculty colleagues to

9. McGrath, "Evangelical Anglicanism," p. 14.

10. Gillian Sumner, "Evangelicalism and Pastoral Ministry," in France and McGrath, *Evangelical Anglicans,* p. 172.

discuss each other's scholarly works in progress. At one point Nicholas Wolterstorff was writing extensively about the philosophy of art, and during a discussion of one of his projects, I asked him to help me understand the intentions of an artist whose work I had recently encountered. This person would cover a good-sized piece of plywood with Elmer's Glue. Then he would take a stringed instrument — the example I saw was a cello — and smash it onto the plywood. When the glue hardened, holding the shattered fragments in place, he would present this to the world as a work of art.

"What is going on there?" I asked Wolterstorff. His answer was a helpful one for me. Whenever we see a puzzling artwork of this sort, he said, we should think of the artist as at least implicitly asking us this question: "OK, would you call *this* a work of art?" — thus inviting us to think about the appropriate categories and boundaries for evaluating aesthetic works.

I think that this kind of question can also help us to understand some recent — and much publicized — developments in evangelical congregational life. In many "seeker sensitive" congregations, Wolterstorff-type questions are being asked about various dimensions of churchly life: "OK, would you call *this* a church building?" "OK, would you call *this* a congregation?" "OK, would you call *this* a worship service?" "OK, would you call *this* a sermon?"

At work here are something like "deconstructionist" tendencies in evangelicalism's ways of thinking about the life and mission of the church. If we are intent upon a continuing program of church renewal, we need to keep our definitions of the forms and patterns of ecclesial life somewhat open-ended. We might even see this fluidity as simply a more radical manifestation of recent ecclesiological developments in the larger church. For example, Avery Dulles, in his now-classic 1974 study of diverse models for understanding the church, draws heavily on Paul Minear's discovery of ninety-six images of the church in the New Testament as a basis for arguing that ecclesiology must be open to the plurality and dynamism of the Bible's depiction of ecclesial reality: "Under the leading of the Holy Spirit," Dulles observes, "the images and forms of Christian life will continue to change, as they have in previous centuries."[11]

11. Avery Dulles, S.J., *Models of the Church: A Critical Assessment of the Church in all its Aspects* (Garden City, N.Y.: Doubleday and Co., 1974), p. 192.

Evangelicals typically defend this ecclesial fluidity in evangelistic terms. "I have become all things to all people," says the apostle, "[so] that I might by all means save some" (1 Cor. 9:22). Needless to say, important consideration must also be given to what the church has to offer people *after* they have been saved. Maturation in Christ, growth in discipleship — these are also important ecclesial concerns. Evangelicals who have been highly "fluid" in reconfiguring congregational life for evangelistic purposes must also pay attention to the crucial role of the church in providing a context for the process of sanctification. But here too we can expect the evangelical patterns to be characterized by a higher degree of open-endedness than would be tolerated in other traditions.

A second feature is the *localist* impulse in evangelical ecclesiology. Although I can touch upon it here only in passing, this is an important topic that needs more attention than it has received. Evangelicalism is often criticized for being too "individualistic," and while this is not totally undeserved, my own sense is that some of those patterns that are seen as individualistic are better thought of as grounded in a deep commitment to the local.

This commitment certainly makes sense in the light of the history of pietism. Ernest Stoeffler's classic account of this history makes it very clear that the common theme in all manifestations of pietism is *experiential Christian fellowship*.[12] Even when pietists chose to remain as members of established churches, and regularly attended corporate worship in cathedral-like contexts, they still supplemented that involvement with "house church" gatherings of small groups of Christians who were devoted to more intimate patterns of devotional Bible study and prayer. Interestingly, this pattern persists in today's evangelical "mega-churches," where Sunday morning services that usually draw thousands of worshipers are supplemented by elaborate "small group" programs.

To be sure, the positive emphasis on intimate spiritual fellowship — which comports well with the pietist call to "a personal faith in Jesus Christ" — is regularly accompanied by rather negative attitudes toward centralized denominational authority. In a profound sense, the Bible best interprets itself for pietists where a few Christians gather for devotional Bible study, challenging each other to discover meanings that are relevant to

12. Cf. F. Ernest Stoeffler, *The Rise of Evangelical Pietism* (Leiden: E. J. Brill, 1965), pp. 9-23.

practical Christian living. Preaching in the local church service is one step removed from this normative context. Bishops, synods, denominational agencies, and theological schools are even further removed. Much of the ethos of North American evangelicalism can be seen as being shaped by this pietist heritage with reinforcement by American pragmatism.

I turn now to a third feature of evangelical ecclesiology: *strong support for "para-church" structures.* Evangelicals have established a variety of trans- and non-denominational institutions and organizations in order to facilitate collective action in what we see as important areas of Christian life and witness. We have founded our own seminaries, liberal arts colleges, Bible institutes, mission agencies, evangelistic associations, Bible distribution societies, and the like — and we have seldom done so along strictly denominational lines. In our own way, then, we evangelicals have been very ecumenical in our eagerness to form liaisons across denominations. To be sure, we have been quite suspicious of the "organizational unity" endeavors of those Christians who are fond of inclusivist councils and denominational mergers. But that merely signals a commitment to a different style of ecumenism, one that emphasizes cooperation in common tasks, such as evangelism and mission.

Recently, Joel Carpenter has told the story of this alternative pattern of organization-building with great sensitivity in his much-acclaimed book, *Revive Us Again: The Reawakening of American Fundamentalism.* Carpenter's narrative begins with the failed efforts of fundamentalists to gain control of denominational structures during their battles with the "modernists" in the first three decades of the twentieth century. Having been forced to the margins of mainstream cultural life, they now saw themselves as a faithful band of believers in a world that was headed for destruction. Their other-worldliness was undergirded by a closely related apocalyptic eschatology and a remnant ecclesiology, and they came to understand their primary mission as evangelism — "rescuing the perishing" and preparing them for heavenly citizenship.

Much of Carpenter's study focuses on the intricate organizational subculture the fundamentalists constructed to implement this mission. While the secularizing elites took it for granted that "the old time religion" was a thing of the past, the fundamentalists were building a complex system of independent organizations: youth ministries, evangelistic teams, summer Bible conferences, and radio programs, just to name a few. This fundamentalist subculture was surprisingly trans-denominational, with participants representing the newer independent "Bible churches" as well as pockets of conservatism within the more established denominational bodies.

During the period when the fundamentalists were building this organizational network, the old-line Protestant bodies seemed content to maintain the more traditional denominational patterns, while also forming more elite "conciliar" ecumenical structures. In all of this, they seemed oblivious to the fact that they were quietly being outflanked by those theological opponents whom they thought they had defeated in earlier battles. As Carpenter puts it, although the process was not very visible for several decades, the fundamentalists — most of whom soon adopted the "evangelical" label — were helping to affect "a major shift among the basic institutional carriers of American religious life." The results are quite obvious today: the old-line "denominations have been losing members, income, and influence while special-purpose, non-denominational religious agencies have grown, multiplied, and taken on increasing importance in shaping and carrying people's religious identity."[13] Carpenter does not want us to miss the irony in all of this:

> Fundamentalists turned to independent ministries in part to compensate for the services they lost when they became disenchanted with the agencies of mainline Protestantism. But by pursuing these survival tactics out on the margins, fundamentalists started a trend that has led to the weakening of the most central and powerful corporate expressions of American religion.[14]

What does all of this mean for people who are interested in the topic of "Church Unity and the Papal Office"? I think that Carpenter's observations about the significance of evangelicalism's para-church network provide an interesting starting point for attempting to answer that question. Evangelicals have been highly successful in forging a grass roots ecumenism that is alive and healthy in a time when other, more "official" ecumenical experiments are floundering. It is unfortunate, for example, that the scholarly discussion of the Promise Keepers phenomenon has often focused almost exclusively on the implications of that movement for an un-

13. Joel Carpenter, *Revive Us Again: The Reawakening of American Fundamentalism* (New York: Oxford University Press, 1997), p. 239.
14. Carpenter, *Revive Us Again*, p. 240.

derstanding of gender issues. Here is another kind of question that deserves to be asked: How in the world did the organizers of those gatherings manage to get so many people to attend? Certainly no mainline Protestant denominational agency — or no conciliar organization — would dare to announce a series of stadium rallies for "ordinary" church members with any hope of filling a good-sized sports arena. In this case evangelicals were able to mobilize communications and organizational resources that made use of a complex network of trans-denominational entities.

I do not offer this example as an exercise in idle partisan boasting. Actually, there *is* someone else in the Christian world who is good at filling large stadiums with crowds of grass roots laity: the pope. And we ought not to ignore this important fact. In a discussion of ecclesial authority it may seem that evangelicals and Roman Catholics are about as far apart as two groups can be on the ecumenical spectrum. But the fact that there are also some interesting similarities should give us some hope that the dialogue is not pointless. Let me discuss, then, a few such similarities — ones that I think are worth sustained examination in ecumenical ecclesiological discussions.

Both Roman Catholicism and evangelicalism have strong populist features. On the face of things, however, it would appear that their populisms function in very different ways. Evangelicalism gives a significant theological voice to the laity. With its doctrine of the perspicuity of Scripture, it often seems to treat the laity's appropriation of biblical teachings as the primary exercise of the church's teaching office — thus creating a great distance from the Catholic insistence on an official magisterial office.

The distance is reduced considerably, though, when we look at some nuances. The notion that the laity's perspective should be taken into account in determining the adequacy of a theological or ethical teaching is certainly not foreign to Catholic thought. While in the past a fairly passive role was assigned to the laity in this regard, Cardinal Newman signaled a new emphasis when he wrote of the importance for church leaders to take seriously "a sort of instinct, or *phronema,* deep in the bosom of the mystical body of Christ."[15] Edmund Dobbin points out in his excellent overview

15. John Henry Cardinal Newman, "On Consulting the Faithful in Matters of Doctrine," in *Conscience, Consensus and the Development of Doctrine: Revolutionary Texts by John Henry Cardinal Newman,* with Commentary and Notes by James Gaffney (New York: Doubleday, 1992), p. 406.

of the topic that before the nineteenth century the preferred term seemed to be *consensus fidelium* rather than *sensus fidelium* — the "consent" rather than the "sense" of ordinary "faithful" believers. The distinction, Dobbin insists, is not a minor one, since "*sensus* refers to the active discerning, or capability of discerning, the content of faith, whereas *consensus* is the 'consensual' result of that discerning."[16]

Not only is there much room in Catholic thought, then, for an active theological discerning role on the part of the laity; there is also an unofficial magisterium that shapes the theological patterns of the evangelical community. Evangelicals sustain a major industry that produces books, audio tapes, television programs, Christian radio stations — all providing considerable commentary on the Bible and its application to daily living. Interestingly, the top acknowledged "teachers" in the evangelical movement are typically elevated to their role by a popular "reception" process that has almost no connection to official ecclesial status. Most evangelicals would be hard put to pass a test in which they were asked to identify the present denominational affiliations of, for example, James Dobson, Charles Colson, Marilyn Hickey, Gary Bauer, Max Lucado, and Pat Robertson. Nonetheless, the combination of evangelical recognition of the need for at least an unofficial teaching office and Roman Catholic support for the role of the laity in the church's discernment process suggests the real possibility of productive dialogue about some interesting subject matter for mutual exploration. Here too we must not be discouraged by an initial contrast between Catholicism's well-defined hierarchical system and evangelicalism's array of loosely structured ministries resisting clear ecclesiological definition.

A few years ago I came across an article in a scholarly journal about a medieval dispute somewhere in the European Low Countries, between a bishop and the abbot of a monastery. The abbot had a knack for drawing parishioners away from the local parishes for a variety of special occasions. Attraction to the monastery was enhanced by regular reports of healings and other manifestations of divine mercy occasioned by those visits. The bishop resented the diversion of financial offerings away from the diocesan coffers. When I read this account I was struck by the parallels to contemporary situations where, say, members of Methodist congregations regu-

16. Edmund Dobbin, "Sensus Fidelium Reconsidered," *New Theology Review* 2:2 (August 1989): 50.

larly attend evangelical-sponsored summer Bible conferences, or where Lutheran youth prefer membership in Young Life clubs to parish-sponsored youth groups.

Or where Catholic parishioners loudly proclaim the spiritual benefits they receive from a large laity-led Wednesday evening Catholic charismatic prayer service that meets in a local high school gymnasium. For the fact is that the world of Catholicism encompasses a wide variety of ecclesial configurations that are not easily defined within the standard categories of Catholic ecclesiology. Disputes between bishops and abbots are not unknown in our own times, and I have sat in on conversations where Catholic theologians struggled to explain the actual lines of authority in such situations in terms of a coherent ecclesiology. Those Catholics who organize themselves to promote an awareness of the Fatima prophecies, or who join Opus Dei, or who send their monthly checks to Mother Angelica are not unlike the evangelicals who support para-church entities.

In the 1980s the theological leaders of the Young Life organization studied their own patterns — conferring with other para-church ministries in the process — in order to clarify for themselves their relationship to what we evangelicals often refer to as "the organized church." Their discussions paid careful attention to a variety of ecclesiological questions. Interestingly, they concluded that their relationship to the institutional churches was much like that of a Catholic religious order to more central ecclesial structures. This suggests that it might be a fascinating bit of bilateral dialogue to have leaders from Young Life, the Moody Bible Institute, and World Vision meet for ecclesiological discussion with representatives of the Franciscans, the Jesuits, and the Sisters of Charity!

The importance of exploring these and related matters is intensified by the increasing patterns of cooperation between evangelicals and Roman Catholics on the grassroots level. One of the most surprising ecumenical developments of the twentieth century is one that seldom gets mentioned by those who construct the narratives of recent ecumenism: what Timothy George has referred to as "the ecumenism of the trenches." The Right to Life movement has been an important instrument in this regard — as have other "culture wars" movements. These partnerships have also fostered dialogue among the laity on other issues of theological and spiritual concern. In an important sense, evangelical and Roman Catholic elites are being challenged to catch up with significant ecumenical discussions that have taken place thus far largely outside of their "official" spheres of influence.

In presenting these thoughts I have focused primarily on evangelicalism's relationship to Roman Catholicism. I have also attempted to present evangelical patterns in a sympathetic light. Before concluding, though, I must also express my deep conviction that a broad-ranging dialogue about these matters — not only with Roman Catholics but also with persons from other Christian traditions — is important for the health of evangelicalism.

Earlier I suggested that the "evangelical" label functions best as a theological modifier rather than as a noun. I worry about a generic evangelicalism that sees itself as an alternative to all other confessional traditions. This is not to retract my earlier endorsement of a set of evangelical emphases and convictions that are espoused by Christians from a variety of denominational and para-church groups. I do believe firmly in the normative authority of the Scriptures, and in the need to proclaim the gospel to all human beings in the hope that many souls will enter into a life-transforming relationship with the crucified and risen Savior.

But I am also strongly convinced that these emphases and convictions function best when they are incorporated into programs of spiritual and theological renewal within the existing confessional traditions. I am deeply grateful, for example, for the increasing number of faithful Roman Catholics and Orthodox Christians who are self-consciously working for evangelical renewal within their faith communities. My gratitude focuses not only on the gifts that they are bringing to their own traditions, but also on the gifts that they bring from those traditions to the evangelical movement.

We evangelicals at our generic worst suffer from theological amnesia. Our narratives about "the old time religion" tend to leave whole centuries — even whole millennia — out of the story of how God has led his church into new understandings of the truth of the gospel. We need conversation partners who will invite us into living communities of memory. When that happens on a large scale, the evangelical movement will be renewed by its life together with the broader Christian community even as it continues to promote its own vision of renewal.

The Church's Teaching Authority and the Call for Democracy in North Atlantic Catholicism

GEORGE WEIGEL

Perhaps the boldest stroke in *Ut Unum Sint,* a singularly bold encyclical, was Pope John Paul II's proposal that Orthodox and Protestant Christians help him conceive an exercise of the Petrine primacy that was "open to a new situation" and that could be of service to them.[1] More than nine hundred years after the break between the Christian East and West, and more than four hundred years after the intra-Western fracture of the Reformation, the bishop of Rome was inviting his separated brethren to think through with him, precisely as Peter's brothers and sisters in Christ, the exercise of Peter's ministry in the church of the third millennium. It was, and remains, a daring, even breathtaking suggestion, certainly one of the most potentially consequential in ecumenical affairs since the Edinburgh Missionary Conference launched the modern ecumenical movement in 1910.

At the same time, it should be candidly admitted that the response from Peter's Orthodox and Protestant brothers and sisters has not been overwhelming. Dr. Konrad Reiser, General Secretary of the World Council of Churches, told a reporter in 1997 that the pope's proposal for a common reflection on how the successor of Peter could exercise a primatial office of unity for the benefit of all Christians "begs the question." The issue, Dr. Reiser argued, was not the exercise of the Petrine office "but the papal primacy itself." That, the secretary general indicated, is "still very difficult

1. John Paul II, *Ut Unum Sint,* No. 95-96.

for me to get hold of." Read through the prism of Dr. Reiser's 1995 proposal that the classic ecumenical search for doctrinal unity be abandoned for the sake of united political action against racism, nationalism, and environmental degradation, the general secretary's reaction to the pope's proposal did not suggest that very much rethinking about the Petrine ministry was likely to come from those quarters where Dr. Reiser's views were considered to be in the theological mainstream.[2]

The response from Orthodoxy has also been tepid. While he did not take up the question of a new exercise of the Petrine primacy in his noteworthy Georgetown University address in October 1997, Ecumenical Patriarch Bartholomew I's contention that the obstacles to the restoration of full communion between Orthodoxy and Roman Catholicism could not be reduced to "a problem of organizational structures [or] jurisdictional arrangements" because "the manner in which we exist has become ontologically different" did not presage the kind of conversation John Paul II evidently envisioned in *Ut Unum Sint*.[3] The ecumenical patriarch has taken pains since the Georgetown lecture to suggest that his reference to "ontologically different" experiences of the church had referred to ways of life rather than essential differences. Still, the complex menu of issues dividing Orthodoxy and Roman Catholicism in Eastern Europe, coupled with the resistance to further Orthodox ecumenical engagement exhibited by influential Orthodox theologians (including the monastic community of Mt. Athos), indicates that John Paul II's vision of an intense Roman Catholic–Orthodox dialogue on the Petrine primacy, perhaps leading to a return to the status quo ante 1054, is indeed a vision for the twenty-first century, and perhaps beyond.

Finally, one could not reasonably expect the pope's proposal to be forthrightly engaged at the present historical moment by the vast majority of evangelical Protestants. Given the prior issues that must be addressed in that dialogue before the question of an apostolically ordered and divinely warranted primacy could be raised intelligibly, it is simply too early for mainstream evangelicalism to wrestle seriously with the issue of the pri-

2. For Reiser on *Ut Unum Sint*, see Gabriel Meyer, "World Council of Churches Chief Counts on Roman Participation," *National Catholic Register*, January 5-11, 1997, p. 5; Reiser's 1994 lecture on the new ecumenism may be found in *Centro Pro Unione Semi-Annual Bulletin* 48 (Fall 1995).

3. Bartholomew I, "Dialogue, from an Orthodox Perspective," *Origins* 27:20 (October 30, 1997): 333, 335-337.

macy, however much many of its leaders may admire the present pope for his public moral witness. As with Orthodoxy, albeit for a different set of reasons, an evangelical–Roman Catholic dialogue in response to John Paul's invitation in *Ut Unum Sint* is an issue for another century.

Unexpected Consequences

Ironically enough, the most vigorous response to the papal proposal to re-think the Petrine primacy in a way that is "open to a new situation" has come from Roman Catholics advocating a particular vision of church re-form. Although they were not the primary addressees of the pope's invita-tion to a new conversation about the primacy and its exercise, these groups and individuals have evidently assumed that any such generous ecumeni-cal overture must extend to them as well. Thus the years since *Ut Unum Sint* have seen groups like "We Are Church" and "Call to Action" and exer-cises like the recent "Delegates Summit" of the "Dialogue for Austria" ap-peal to *Ut Unum Sint,* Nos. 95-96, or to the spirit of the encyclical as a war-rant for advancing their claims.

Perhaps most substantively, Archbishop John R. Quinn, the retired Archbishop of San Francisco and former president of the National Confer-ence of Catholic Bishops (NCCB), explicitly appealed to *Ut Unum Sint* in a widely publicized lecture, "Considerations of the Papacy," which he deliv-ered at Oxford's Campion Hall on June 29, 1995, a month after the encycli-cal's publication.[4] In that lecture Archbishop Quinn, while not explicitly advocating the kind of doctrinal and disciplinary changes advanced by "Call to Action," "We Are Church," and the Austrian "Delegates Summit," nonetheless seemed to agree with these self-conscious Catholic "progres-sives" on two points: (1) that something is seriously awry in the contempo-rary functioning of the Petrine primacy, and (2) that the evolution of a more democratic form of ecclesial governance is essential for meeting the demands of being the church in the modern world. The warm reception given the archbishop's lecture by *Commonweal, America,* and similarly sit-uated Catholic opinion journals, a reception widely disseminated through the secular press, suggested that Archbishop Quinn was speaking for a

4. John R. Quinn, "Considering the Papacy," *Origins* 26:8 (July 18, 1996): 119-127. The citations to follow are all from this text.

considerable body of opinion among intellectuals, theologians, and church professionals in the Catholic Church in the United States. Here, too, one frequently encounters calls for a more "democratic" church polity, to which the Petrine ministry as presently understood and exercised is thought to be an obstacle.

Archbishop Quinn's lecture — its reading of the signs of the times, its theological argumentation, and its specific proposals — is thus a useful tool for analyzing in its more developed form the call for "democracy" in North Atlantic Catholicism and its relationship to the quest for Christian unity. We know that the concrete functioning of the papacy, as well as the church's understanding of the Petrine ministry, have evolved over time. In the context of *Ut Unum Sint*, the question Archbishop Quinn and others are raising is how the call for a more "democratic" Catholicism bears on the development of doctrine and on the prospects for a form of primacy capable of serving Orthodox and Protestant Christians. At first blush, the Quinn lecture and the proposals it advances may seem promising, as they address questions of structure and polity that have long caused anxieties in the ecumenical context. Indeed, Archbishop Quinn himself quite explicitly suggested that the structural changes he was advocating in the exercise of the Petrine primacy were part of the "price" that the Catholic Church should be willing to pay for ecclesial reunion. On closer examination though, the Quinn proposals and the ecclesiological sensibility they embody are, I suggest, deeply problematic for ecumenism — if by the ecumenical task we mean recomposing in concrete historical form the unity given once-for-all by Christ to the church, which is a unity in the truth that is also given by Christ to the church and guaranteed by the abiding presence of the Holy Spirit in the church.

The Quinn Proposals

As he freely admitted, Archbishop Quinn's specific proposals on a restructured exercise of the primacy were not very original. What may have made them seem fresh was that the archbishop described them as expressions of the Catholic social-ethical concept of "subsidiarity." First given authoritative form by Pope Pius XI in the 1931 encyclical *Quadragesimo Anno,* the principle of subsidiarity (an expression of the Catholic view of society as an organic, not merely contractual reality) holds that decision making should be left at the lowest possible level in a social hierarchy, commensurate with the achievement of the common good. Archbishop Quinn proposed to adopt this principle, which had long been applied to the right ordering of states, to the church from within.

In this context, one target of Archbishop Quinn's criticism of the current exercise of the Petrine primacy was the pope's central staff, the Roman Curia. The Curia, Quinn proposed, had come to think of itself as a *tertium quid*, exercising "oversight and authority over the college of bishops" and seeing itself "as subordinate to the pope but superior to the college of bishops." "To the degree that this is so," Quinn argued, "it obscures and diminishes both the doctrine and the reality of episcopal collegiality." Among the examples adduced were the Curia's alleged interference in the publication of the English edition of the *Catechism of the Catholic Church*, and what the archbishop described as a lack of "consultation" with local bishops prior to "doctrinal and other important pronouncements" from the dicasteries of the Roman Curia.

As a remedy to this alleged curiacentrism in contemporary church governance, Archbishop Quinn proposed four structural changes in Catholic polity. The Synod of Bishops should be reconstituted as a deliberative assembly, a kind of church parliament, exercising a legislative function parallel to the pope's executive responsibilities.[5] Ecumenical councils of all the world's bishops ought to be summoned far more regularly; and while the archbishop did not advocate a fixed time period, his one historical reference in this regard was to the Council of Constance's fifteenth century proposal that an ecumenical council be summoned every ten years. In the third place, Archbishop Quinn proposed that the national conferences of bishops established since Vatican II exercise some form of magisterial function, arguing that the conferences should be "seriously consulted . . . before doctrinal declarations are issued or binding decisions made of a disciplinary or liturgical nature." Finally, the archbishop proposed that bishops be nominated by local churches and national episcopal conferences, rather than by recommendation of a country's papal nuncio or ap-

---

5. Or, as Archbishop Quinn put it, "It would make the Synod more truly a collegial act if the Synod had a deliberative vote and not merely a consultative vote." The archbishop did not discuss the theological question of how a subset of bishops, no matter how chosen, could make decisions binding on individual bishops, or what such an exercise in representative ecclesiastical democracy would do to the teaching authority of the local bishop, which in other parts of his lecture Archbishop Quinn was eager to enhance.

ostolic delegate to the Congregation for Bishops (which then makes recommendations to the pope).

In addition, and with specific reference to the function of the Petrine primacy *stricte dictu,* the archbishop suggested that future popes should be far more restrained in exercising the papal teaching office. While not explicit, the phrase "than this Pope has been" seems implicit here, the chief reference point being John Paul II's 1994 apostolic letter *Ordinatio Sacerdotalis* on the church's inability to ordain women to the ministerial priesthood. While granting the right of the pope "to teach on his own initiative as he sees fit," Archbishop Quinn argues that the "real issue is when and under what circumstances he should prudently exercise such a right." Great attention has been paid, the archbishop suggested, to the doctrinal aspects of the primacy, and too little to "the place of prudence in the exercise of the primacy." The question, it may be assumed, would not have been pressed so vigorously had the archbishop believed that the "place of prudence in the exercise of the primacy" was well understood, or that prudence had been a hallmark of recent papal teaching.

Reading the "New Situation"

Archbishop Quinn offered his proposals as a response to the "new situation" to which Pope John Paul II referred in *Ut Unum Sint.* Thus the first questions to be asked follow naturally: What is the archbishop's rendering of the relevant "signs of the times," and does that rendering coincide with the "new situation" as understood by John Paul II when he suggested rethinking the exercise of the primacy in response to these phenomena?

In parsing the "new situation," Archbishop Quinn made brief and welcome reference to "the insistent thirst for unity among Christians" and to post-conciliar Catholicism's renewed sense of every Christian's baptismal dignity and evangelical responsibility. But the archbishop's primary reference points for locating the "new situation" were political, economic, social, technological, and psychological: the collapse of communism, the emergence of China as a major world power, the quest for European unity, the women's movement, worldwide resistance to authoritarianism, the gap between rich and poor, large numbers of refugees, the marginalization of Africa, and the loss of large numbers of Catholics to "sects or non-Christian religions." In addition, Archbishop Quinn suggested, there is a "new psychology" with which the church must contend, in which "people think differently, react differently, have new aspirations, a new sense of what is possible, new hopes and dreams."

Some of these are, undoubtedly, important and interesting facts of life at the turn of the century. But in thinking through a Petrine primacy for the third millennium, one has to ask whether these facts are as crucial or as relevant as certain other realities, regularly identified as the crucial "signs of the times" by John Paul II's theologically driven vision of history:

- the *reductio ad absurdum* of the two-hundred-year-old effort to define human freedom as radical autonomy from any moral tradition or moral community;
- the logical and lethal workings-out of this "autonomy project" in abortion-on-demand and physician-assisted suicide, understood as basic human rights;
- the birth of vibrant Christian communities throughout Asia and Africa;
- the challenge of militant Islam;
- the emergence of culturally assertive evangelical and pentecostal Protestant communities in the Americas, eastern Europe, and Asia;
- the explosion of renewal movements in Catholicism throughout the world, and the emergence of new forms of consecrated life;
- the possibility of a more theologically serious Jewish-Christian dialogue than at any time since the first-century "parting of the ways";
- the fact that ours is the greatest century of martyrdom in Christian history.

Responding to these signs of the times and this "new situation," John Paul II has taken Luke 22:32 with utmost seriousness, and has reconstituted an evangelical papacy for the twenty-first century by returning the exercise of the Petrine primacy to its New Testament roots: Peter as the church's first witness to God's saving action in Jesus Christ, Peter as the evangelist whose singular responsibility is to strengthen his brethren in their own evangelization. In effecting this radically evangelical reconstruction of the papacy — and I use "radically" here in the twin sense of "deeply rooted" and "boldly innovative" — John Paul II has made the church's presence known on the world-historical stage in a way that it has not been for centuries.

This combination of biblical retrieval and historical "presence" is of considerable consequence for understanding the primacy and its exercise in the future. And it involves a rather different identification of the "signs of the times" than those highlighted by Archbishop Quinn's lecture. In responding to the new situation created by the crisis of humanism in the twentieth century, John Paul II has created a new situation for the primacy. That new situation seems inadequately appreciated by those pressing an agenda of ecclesiastical reconstruction that is a response to a different reading of the signs of the times, a reading that leads to a different sense of Christian possibility in the world.

The Denominational Temptation

In making his proposals for restructuring the central administration of the Catholic Church, Archbishop Quinn argued that his was an "ecclesial" model of governance in sharp contrast to the "political" model he found dominant today in Rome. Yet one of the most striking things about the archbishop's "ecclesial" model is that it is intensely bureaucratic. Indeed, were they put into practice, the archbishop's proposals would likely create a bureaucratization of Catholicism beyond the wildest dreams of the most ultramontane Roman curialist.

The Quinn proposals suggest an application on a world scale of the practices adopted by the U.S. bishops in their national conference — practices that were themselves influenced by the example of modern Protestant church bureaucracies in America. Archbishop Quinn suggested that the universal application of this model would make for a more effective expression of the individual bishop's local authority and the world episcopate's collegiality. Yet judging by the NCCB's experience over the past thirty years, it seems likely that the first and most immediate impact of the Quinn proposals on the episcopate would be that bishops would find themselves dragooned into even more meetings — an aspect of their lives about which many of these men vociferously and legitimately complain already. A bishop's life today is already replete with administrative chores. When, it might be asked, will bishops have time for evangelization and teaching if their working days are further consumed by attending to the appointment of other bishops, preparing for legislative synods, and taking part in frequent ecumenical councils?

Archbishop Quinn is eager to enhance the authority of local bishops, but the dynamics of the NCCB as it presently functions suggest that the very opposite of strengthened subsidiarity and collegiality would result if the archbishop's proposals for devolving even more decision-making authority onto local episcopal conferences were implemented. Because of the bishops' concern to maintain their unity as a national body and their commitment to a "consensus" style of decision making, small, vocal, ideologically charged minorities now exercise power within the conference far beyond their numbers — a clear diminishment of both the collegial authority of the conference and the authority of individual bishops. The bishops' corporate and individual authority has also been whittled away by the rise of a "parallel magisterium" of conference officials and bureaucrats, whose ability to shape agendas and decide what it is that the bishops must decide strikes many as a far cry from collegiality.

The American experience of major teaching documents prepared by the bishops' conference should also give more pause than Archbishop Quinn allows. The Revolution of 1989 in Eastern and Central Europe made clear that the 1983 national pastoral letter, "The Challenge of Peace," had seriously misread the dynamics of contemporary history and the path to peace and freedom. The 1986 national pastoral letter, "Economic Justice for All," was quickly superseded by the far more creative 1991 papal encyclical, *Centesimus Annus.* The inability of the bishops to reach agreement on a pastoral letter on women in the church and society was an embarrassing affair that should have raised caution flags about the capture of the conference's attention and agenda by a small cadre determined to stretch the boundaries of doctrine and practice through the instrument of a national pastoral letter.

The history of post–World War II mainline Protestantism in America is a cautionary sign of the times to which Archbishop Quinn and those of his persuasion pay insufficient attention. The demographic implosion of mainline Protestantism has taken place parallel to, and maybe even because of, both the bureaucratization of those churches and the capture of denominational bureaucracies by activists committed to a theological and political agenda whose linkage to the great tradition of Christian orthodoxy is not, to be gentle, self-evidently clear. It hardly seems plausible to suggest that this is the path Catholicism should follow; no doubt Archbishop Quinn and at least some of his supporters would deny that this is in fact where they want the church to go. Yet the dynamics of bureaucratization have a certain universality to them, as Max Weber taught us long ago, and it would be foolhardy to suggest that Catholicism is immune to their effects. These sociological concerns about the kind of "democratic" church envisioned by Archbishop Quinn and his supporters ought to be taken seriously by Orthodox and Protestant Christians trying to respond to John Paul II's invitation to help rethink the functioning of the Petrine primacy. What is sometimes too readily dismissed as the "merely sociological" can have a profound impact on the church's capacity to evangelize and serve the world.

There are also theological issues of considerable gravity engaged here. Archbishop Quinn's proposals seem deeply influenced by the American experience of the church as a voluntary association. As Tocqueville famously observed, the voluntary association is a very American thing, and indeed a very good thing. There is certainly nothing intrinsically un-Catholic about a voluntary association. On the contrary, voluntary associations, especially those with social-welfare concerns, are among the most important ways in which American civil society embodies the principle of subsidiarity and what the 1991 encyclical *Centesimus Annus* called the "subjectivity of society."[6] But it should also be understood that, within the mainline Protestant culture that so powerfully shaped American self-understanding and social experience until the Second World War, "voluntary association" was a sociological reality that carried heavy theological baggage with it. The national experience of the voluntary association, for example, implied the church as denomination, and American Christianity came to be understood by the majority culture as denominational Christianity. Thus to be religious in America meant, for the great majority, to belong to a denomination and to think "denominationally." Indeed, this cultural expectation was so strong that it had a powerful effect on the most ancient religious traditions, as illustrated by the Reform movement's early attempts to turn Judaism into yet another denomination.

This experience of denominational Christianity poses serious problems for Catholics, and indeed for any doctrinally and ecclesially serious Christian. In denominational Christianity, there is little that is given or secure about the ecclesial community; rather, the church is constantly being remade by its members. The church as denomination has no distinctive or fixed "form" (in the Balthasarian sense) given to it by Christ; it adapts its

6. See John Paul II, *Centesimus Annus*, No. 13, 46.

"form" (understood in external terms, as its institutional structures) to the patterns of the age. As lived out in mainline American Protestantism since World War II, denominationalism has also meant that bureaucratic "process" is more important than binding doctrinal reference points; that the boundaries of the community are ill-defined and porous; that institutional maturity requires extensive bureaucratization; and that the charism of religious leadership equals the "skill" of bureaucratic management. Most basically, while a denomination is something we create by joining it, the church, according to the ancient tradition reaffirmed by Vatican II, is a divinely ordered and Spirit-sustained reality, born from the blood and water of the Cross, into which we are incorporated by sacraments of initiation.

The question of the transformation of religious leadership by the conscious adoption or unconscious assumption of a denominational ecclesiology should, of course, be of particular interest to those like Archbishop Quinn, who rightly insist that the local bishop is not a branch manager of Roman Catholic Church, Inc. The historical record seems to indicate, however, that the bureaucratization attendant upon a denominational concept and experience of the church inexorably attenuates the unique character of the office of bishop, with its singular combination of doctrinal and juridical authority. The early church may have adopted the terms "bishop" (ἐπίσκοπος or "overseer") and "diocese" from the surrounding public culture. But from the beginning, the episcopate was a uniquely *ecclesial* office and the charisms necessary to fulfill its obligations were evangelical and theological — in a word, religious. This stands in sharpest contrast to what much of American Christianity has come to understand as a "denominational leader." The latter's charism, or, better, "skill," is managerial, even bureaucratic. His or her authority does not derive from ordination, but from election in a political process in which a premium is placed on balancing the various factions and interests within the denomination. Furthermore, at least in daily practice, the principal reference point for the work of the denominational leader is the denominational staff, or bureaucracy. None of this represents an enhancement of the authority of the episcopate. Instead it represents a serious — some would say, drastic — distortion of the episcopal office.

Given the realities of religious choice in the modern world, Catholicism in the twenty-first century will most certainly be a voluntary association, sociologically described. But the temptation to "denominationalize" the church's self-understanding and exercise of its teaching authority must

be resisted, for "Catholic" and "denominational" are theological ant-
onyms. The sensibility that seems to inform Archbishop Quinn's proposals
and other attempts to make Catholicism more "democratic" does not seem
sufficiently attentive to this problem. That should raise serious questions
in the minds of Orthodox and Protestant ecumenists interested in a unity
founded on the truth once delivered to the saints.

Collegiality and Primacy

The Quinn lecture and similar proposals for a more "democratic" Catholicism also do not adequately address the relationship of collegiality and the
Petrine primacy, which are of obvious and considerable interest to ecumenically minded Orthodox and Protestant Christians. According to *Lumen
Gentium,* the *Dogmatic Constitution on the Church* of Vatican II, the college
of bishops and the Petrine primacy within the college are both divinely ordered and constitutive elements of the church.[7] They are to be exercised together in ways that strengthen the church's essential character, its *communio.* Because both primacy and collegiality serve that *communio,* the
relationship between them must be understood *sui generis,* and not by primary reference to other models of governance, especially political models.

The Quinn proposals seem to treat the relationship of primacy and
collegiality as a kind of zero-sum exercise, in which primacy (or the effective exercise thereof) must diminish as collegiality increases. But this is to
confuse the relationship between the pope and the members of the episcopal college with the relationship between management and labor in the
negotiation of a new union contract, 1930s-style. If both primacy and collegiality are of the will of Christ, then they ought not be seen or function in
such a way that enhancing one element necessitates diminishing the other.

It is also worth asking whether this zero-sum model of the relationship takes sufficient account of Vatican II's insistence that collegiality is always effectively exercised with the Petrine primacy, rather than against it,
in competition with it, or as an alternative to it. In a genuinely Vatican II
model, it would seem that the national episcopal conferences, instruments
of collegiality to which Archbishop Quinn and others give great weight,
should actively seek the approbation of the bishop of Rome for their colle-

7. See *Lumen Gentium,* No. 22-24.

gial acts, especially those with the greatest theological, liturgical, or disciplinary impact. Such approbation, Cardinal Francis George has suggested, would give those acts a fullness of authority that is not present when a local collegial action is not confirmed by the head of the college. Such an approach, it should be added, puts the 1998 apostolic letter on episcopal conferences, *Apostolos Suos,* in an entirely different light, for its suggests that true acts of collegiality by national conferences of bishops are magnified, not diminished, by the approval they receive from the Apostolic See.

A theological rather than managerial-political approach would also help us think through the right relationship between the local bishop and the national bishops' conferences on the one hand, and the Roman Curia as an instrument of the Petrine primacy on the other. In proposing an international commission to design a reform of the Roman Curia, Archbishop Quinn suggested that such a commission should "consult experts in management, government, theology, canon law, and other useful disciplines and professions." The order of expertise to be sought here is instructive. The priority given to "experts in management [and] government" would not seem to presage a genuinely ecclesial exploration of these relationships and their reform. Why, one wonders, does the theology not come first?[8]

Prudence and the Primacy

That the virtue of prudence should inform the exercise of the primacy and its teaching authority is, or ought to be, a given. An effective deployment of the papal magisterium is, among other things, an exercise in the discernment of a *kairos,* a moment when it is ripe to speak. John Paul II's bold proclamation of Christian humanism in *Redemptor Hominis* and *Evangelium Vitae,* his creative extension of Catholic social doctrine in *Centesimus Annus,* his summons to a new evangelization and a method of evangelical persuasion in *Redemptoris Missio,* his profoundly christological reading of history and his unprecedented call for ecclesial repentance in

8. As it did not, unfortunately, in the design of the U.S. bishops' conference by the management-consultant firm of Booz, Allen, and Hamilton. See Thomas J. Reese, *A Flock of Shepherds: The National Conference of Catholic Bishops* (Kansas City: Sheed and Ward, 1992), pp. 81-84.

Tertio Millennio Adveniente, his defense of the universality of human rights in his two U.N. addresses, and his defense of human reason in *Fides et Ratio* all suggest that this pontificate has been replete with a sense of *kairos.* But these are not the issues in which Archbishop Quinn was interested in his Oxford lecture (indeed, these documents are never mentioned there). Nor are these the issues that most engage the attention of those Catholics calling for a more "democratic" church. Rather, running subtly through the Quinn lecture, as it runs openly through activist circles in the Catholic Church in the United States, is the suggestion that the 1994 apostolic letter *Ordinatio Sacerdotalis,* which declared that the church had no authority to ordain women to the ministerial priesthood, was, to adopt Archbishop Quinn's language, a "circumstance" in which a "prudent" pope would not have exercised his "right to teach on his own initiative."

It is difficult to understand the argument from prudence here. A prudent leader does not encourage speculation about the impossible. Rather, he clearly identifies the boundaries of the discussion so that attention can be focused on real and achievable reforms. That, I believe, is what John Paul II intended to do in *Ordinatio Sacerdotalis.* By defining the boundaries of the possible, the pope cleared the ground for a more fruitful, and perhaps far more radical, discussion about the declericalization of Catholic life and the depoliticization of the ministerial priesthood.[9] In doing so, he was acting as an authoritative teacher, the custodian and servant of a tradition, not as an authoritarian imposing his personal opinions on the church. Archbishop Quinn would have helped dispel one of the great myths about contemporary Catholicism had he pointed that out.

A New Agenda

To take a critical stance toward many "democratization" proposals in contemporary Catholicism is not to suggest that there is not room for real re-

---

9. Whether this end would have been better served had *Ordinatio Sacerdotalis* not been framed as a papal reaffirmation of the 1976 statement from the Congregation for the Doctrine of the Faith, *Inter Insigniores,* but rather laid out a more developed statement on the theology of the priesthood, drawing on the sacramental and iconographic themes developed in John Paul II's theology of the body, is another question. I address this question in my book *Witness to Hope: The Biography of Pope John Paul II* (New York: HarperCollins, 1999).

form in Catholic polity and in the concrete practice of the church's governance. The process currently used at the Synod of Bishops is in need of serious review.[10] It might also be suggested that the practice of drawing many senior appointments in the Roman Curia from the ranks of the papal diplomatic service, as a matter of course, deserves reconsideration. The church's diplomats are, as a body, a group of extremely skilled and dedicated men. Some of those skills are transferable to certain dicasteries of the Roman Curia, but in other instances both the internal curial process and the church as a whole arguably would be better served by the appointment of residential bishops to senior leadership positions. Then there is the question of the further internationalization of the Curia, in which the break with a certain cultural pattern of "the way we do things here" must reach deeper into the membership.

The church's doctrinal and disciplinary boundaries are defined by an authoritative tradition of which the pastors of the church and its theologians are servants, not masters. This by no means precludes the development of doctrine, the reform of discipline, or the restructuring of the church's polity. In the church understood as a *communio,* however, the development of doctrine and practice takes place primarily through prayer, discernment, theological reflection that reflects the demands of both *ressourcement* and *aggiornamento,* and a distinctly ecclesial form of deliberation. An authentically ecclesial development of doctrine and practice may involve organizing, lobbying, and the marshaling of factions into a consensus, but these are not the primary modalities of a truly ecclesial discernment. From the Detroit "Call to Action" conference in 1976 through the transatlantic petition campaign of "We Are Church" and on to the 1998 Austrian Delegates Summit, a distinctively ecclesial process of discernment was notably absent. While the national conferences of bishops have not been so doctrinally or disciplinarily adventurous as these activist movements, I would suggest respectfully but realistically that they have a considerable way to go before they begin to function in a distinctively ecclesial and episcopal way. A meeting of bishops that closely resembles in style and process a meeting of a corporate board of directors is probably not what most of the Fathers of Vatican II meant by collegiality.

Protestant and Orthodox Christians committed to taking seriously

10. For one man's experience of the process, see Richard John Neuhaus, *Appointment in Rome: The Church in America Awakening* (New York: Crossroad, 1999).

Pope John Paul II's invitation in sections 95-96 of *Ut Unum Sint* will, of course, bring different concerns to bear in evaluating the various "democratization" proposals in North Atlantic Catholicism. Protestants deeply concerned about the doctrinal deconstruction of their communities over the past fifty years and committed to recovering the apostolic tradition of the historic episcopate will rightly be concerned about such exercises as the Salzburg "Delegates Summit," which seemed to replicate the procedures (and many of the results) of similar postwar mainline Protestant conclaves. Protestant Christians may also be justifiably concerned about the rather accommodating attitude toward expansive local and national church bureaucracies that seems to inform Archbishop Quinn's proposals. Christians in the Orthodox tradition will welcome the recovery of something like a synodal principle in Roman Catholicism, although, like many Roman Catholic bishops, they may have questions about the way that synods and episcopal conferences function in concrete reality. Of far more ecumenical consequence, however, is the notion embodied in the activist "democratization" movements that doctrine and ecclesiastical discipline are the subject of politically charged legislative processes in which Western notions of "representation" dominate the formation of the decision-making body. This is not, to put it gently, a model of polity that Orthodoxy will find it easy to accept, even in a "sister church."

For ecumenically serious Orthodox and Protestant Christians, as for Catholics formed in the tradition of Vatican II as authentically interpreted by John Paul II, the question most sharply posed by the "democratization" movements is that of the nature of doctrine and its relationship to the *communio* of the church. While the Lord's promise of the Spirit's abiding presence in the church is a guarantee that the *sensus fidelium*, over time, will not fall into fundamental error, "majority rule," understood in contemporary political terms, has not proven a barrier to certain parts of the Οἰκουμένη falling into error at certain moments in history. Moreover, the experience of the past sixty years, primarily in mainline Protestantism but in Catholicism as well, suggests that modern bureaucratic processes and patterns of church governance that emulate state legislatures are not well-fitted to defend or develop doctrine.

Thus an ecumenical conversation about the way in which the church reflects upon and develops its doctrinal and disciplinary life is certainly worthwhile and much needed. That conversation should respectfully engage the proposals being made by the "democratization" movement in

North Atlantic Catholicism without accepting the movement's premise that, because of the pressures and demands of modernity, it is inevitably the shape of the future. Moreover, in that ecumenical conversation, it will be useful to remember that one function of the Petrine primacy is to remind the church, in and out of season, that it is the church, the mystical body of Christ extending over time and space, and that as such its essential structure is sacramental, not political.

Ecumenism and the New Evangelization
in *Ut Unum Sint*

JOSEPH AUGUSTINE DINOIA, O.P.

"Believers in Christ . . . cannot remain divided. If they wish truly and effectively to oppose the world's tendency to reduce to powerlessness the mystery of Redemption, they must profess together the same truth about the cross" (*Ut Unum Sint* [hereafter *UUS*], §1).

Your Eminence, Cardinal Cassidy; your Excellency, Bishop Dudley; brothers and sisters; friends all in Christ. Thanks to Robert Jenson for your kind words of introduction. I can assure you that it is a privilege to address all of you gathered here at the University of St. Thomas for this splendid symposium on "Church Unity and the Papal Office," jointly sponsored by the Center for Catholic and Evangelical Theology and the Archdiocese of St. Paul/Minneapolis. I want to acknowledge publicly the great debt we all owe to Carl Braaten and Robert Jenson for all they have done to bring us together in these days and on many occasions in the past in pursuit of the full and visible unity for which we long.

"Believers in Christ . . . cannot remain divided. . . . How could they refuse to do everything possible . . . to overcome obstacles and prejudices which thwart the proclamation of the Gospel of salvation in the cross of Jesus, the one Redeemer of Man?" (*UUS*, §1,2). It is appropriate in the setting of this conference on the papal office to explore the connection between ecumenism and evangelization. Pope John Paul II, like his predecessors, understands it to be an essential element in the exercise of Petrine ministry to foster unity as an instrument of evangelization. In *Ut Unum*

159

Sint the Holy Father quotes a striking passage from Paul VI's *Evangelii Nuntiandi:* "The destiny of evangelization is certainly bound up with the witness of unity given by the Church. We wish to emphasize the sign of unity among all Christians as a way and instrument of evangelization" (*UUS,* §98; *Evangelii Nuntiandi,* §69). This is a theme already strongly asserted by the Fathers of the Second Vatican Council: division, they wrote in *Unitatis Redintegratio,* "openly contradicts the will of Christ, provides a stumbling block to the world, and inflicts damage on the most holy cause of proclaiming the good news to every creature" (§1). The theme is also thoroughly discussed in the 1993 *Directory on Ecumenism.*

Let us consider how the link between ecumenical commitment and the new evangelization are developed in *Ut Unum Sint.* We need briefly to consider first the main feature of what Father Avery Dulles has aptly termed "the evangelical turn" in recent papal and conciliar teaching. When we view the church's ecumenical commitment in the broad perspective of the new evangelization, we will discover two things: the inherently ecumenical character of the new evangelization and the evangelical challenge to our renewed ecumenism.

The Evangelical Turn in Recent Catholic Teaching

Father Dulles traces the remote origins of "the evangelical turn" in the twentieth century to Karl Barth's emphasis on the need for a renewed proclamation to address the increasing secularization of Western society. More immediately in the Catholic Church, according to Dulles, it was Pope John XXIII's acquaintance with kerygmatic theology when he served as papal nuncio to France that led him to stress the role of evangelization and to make the renewal of evangelization central to the agenda of the Second Vatican Council.

As Dulles points out, although missionary activity has always been part of the church's ministry, the designation of this activity as evangelization is new. Catholics were more likely to describe missionary activity as "the propagation of the faith" or the "establishment of the church." At Vatican II, the church embraced the biblical language of proclaiming with authority and power the good news of Jesus Christ in order to describe her essential mission. Dulles believes that the relative neglect of this aspect of Vatican II's teaching in the immediate aftermath of the Council

160

led Pope Paul VI to devote the 1974 synod to this theme and then to issue the apostolic exhortation *Evangelii Nuntiandi*. Pope John Paul II, who as bishop attended that synod, has embraced the new evangelization and promoted it vigorously throughout his pontificate. Taken together with *Evangelii Nuntiandi*, Pope John Paul's encyclical *Redemptoris Missio* constitutes the great charter of the "new evangelization."

The New Evangelization

Father Dulles, whose writings have contributed so much to alerting English-speaking readers to the centrality of the theme of new evangelization in the program of Pope John Paul II, identifies ecumenism as only one of its ten principal traits. We should consider the other traits briefly before proceeding to ecumenism.

Most important among these traits of the new evangelization are the centrality of Christ and the primacy of the Holy Spirit. The new evangelization is christocentric in that its chief objective is to proclaim Jesus Christ as savior and to foster personal relationships with him. In the work of evangelization the Holy Spirit is the primary agent, both in moving and sustaining the evangelizer and in engendering faith in the hearts of those who hear the message. In addition, according to Dulles, the new evangelization is biblical (in being rooted in and shaped by the Holy Scripture), comprehensive (in embracing the phases of first evangelization, continuing evangelization, and re-evangelization), dialogic (in respecting the freedom of conscience of the hearers), cultural (in its commitment to the transformation of cultures and societies), and innovative (in its readiness to employ new media of communication). Finally, the new evangelization is the responsibility of all Christians, not just the priests and religious who are members of missionary societies, and it must be directed to the members of the church themselves. It is essential to locate the church's recommitment to ecumenism within this broad context of the revitalization of her entire evangelizing mission. For "the Church seeks nothing for herself but the freedom to proclaim the Gospel" (*UUS*, §3).

The Place of Ecumenism in the New Evangelization

In *Ut Unum Sint*, Pope John II can be understood to affirm that it is impossible fully to embrace the new evangelization without committing oneself to ecumenism — to the goal of the visible unity of all the followers of Christ. Noting that "the ecumenical movement in our century . . . has been characterized by a missionary outlook," the pope underscores the significant conjunction of two clauses in Christ's prayer for unity: "That all may be one . . . so that the world may believe that you sent me" (*UUS*, §98). God wills unity; thus "unity stands at the heart of Christ's mission" (*UUS*, §9). At the same time, unity is essential to the effective proclamation of the gospel. If we are committed to the new evangelization, we must be committed to ecumenism: "How can we proclaim the gospel of reconciliation without at the same time being committed to working for reconciliation between Christians?" (*UUS*, §98). It is clear, then, that a lively commitment to ecumenism is crucial both to the *effectiveness* of evangelization, and to the *essence* of evangelization.

Without question, division among Christians is an obstacle to evangelization. It undermines our capacity convincingly to proclaim the truth about the one savior of mankind if we cannot all agree and be seen to agree about what that truth entails. The greater the visible unity among Christians, the more effective will their efforts at evangelizing be.

But — and perhaps even more importantly — commitment to ecumenism touches on the very essence of the message that is at the heart of the new evangelization. "Ecumenism is not only an internal question of the Christian communities. It is a matter of the love which God has in Jesus Christ for all humanity." (*UUS*, §99) Pope John Paul II makes this point quite clearly in the crucial paragraph 9 of *Ut Unum Sint*: "The faithful are one because in the Spirit they are in communion with the Son, and in him share in his communion with the Father. . . . The communion of Christians is none other than the manifestation in them of the grace by which God makes them sharers in his own communion."

At the core of the message of the new evangelization is the divine desire to share the communion of trinitarian life with creaturely persons. What Christ taught us, and we must in turn proclaim to the world, is that the triune God invites all human persons to participate in the communion of the Father, Son, and Holy Spirit, and to enjoy communion with one another in them. Creation, incarnation, redemption: the central mysteries of the Christian faith find their deepest meaning in this divine invitation. Everything created exists so that the Blessed Trinity could realize this plan of love. Through the incarnation and the paschal mystery, Christ enables creaturely persons to enter into the life of the uncreated persons: in the elevation of human nature, the creaturely limits to participation in the divine life are overcome; in the restoration of human nature, the obstacles of sin are removed. The tradition speaks of our "adoptive participation" in the life of the Trinity through Christ: the one who is Son by nature makes it possible for us to be sons and daughters by adoption. This work of the Blessed Trinity in us can be said to "reverse" the order of the processions: whereas in the inner life of the Trinity, the Father loves the Son and gives rise to the Spirit, in the saving work of the Trinity, the Spirit remakes us in the image of the Son so that we may be embraced in the love of the Father.

If we are not committed to ecumenism, we have failed to grasp the heart of the message we must proclaim to one another and to the wide world in the new evangelization. It is a message of communion and love. As St. Irenaeus wrote, "He who has no need of anyone gave communion with himself to those who need him." Thus, Pope John Paul is saying to us that, if we understand the central truth at the heart of the new evangelization and we want to be as effective as possible in communicating that truth to the world, then we must be committed as well to working for the full visible unity of Christians. Thus, as to both effectiveness and essence, a commitment to ecumenism inheres in the work of the new evangelization.

The Evangelical Challenge to Ecumenical Commitment

I believe that *Ut Unum Sint* also has something to say about the ways in which our embrace of the new evangelization shapes our understanding and pursuit of ecumenism. In other words, *Ut Unum Sint* not only teaches us about the inherently ecumenical character of the new evangelization; it also poses an evangelical challenge to the kind of ecumenism we pursue.

A central aspect of the new evangelization in Pope John Paul's conception and practice is that, to be really effective, it must proclaim the full truth about Christ without compromise. It must be, in a sense, unapologetic and unaccommodating. It should not refuse to take people's questions and concrete circumstances into account, but its thrust should be to present the entirety of the gospel with the presumption of its entire truth

163

and intelligibility. The need for effective evangelization to embrace and communicate the entire truth of the gospel is echoed at various points in *Ut Unum Sint*. Consider these striking passages:

18 The unity willed by God can be attained only by the adherence of all to the content of revealed faith in its entirety. In matters of faith, compromise is in contradiction with God who is Truth. . . . A being together which betrayed the truth would thus be opposed to the nature of God who offers his communion and to the need for truth found in the depths of every human heart.

26 GS 24: "The Lord Jesus, when he prayed to the Father 'that all may be one . . . as we are one' opened up vistas closed to human reason. For he implied a certain likeness between the union of the Divine persons, and the union of God's children in truth and charity."

33 In the Council's thinking, ecumenical dialogue is marked by a common quest for truth, particularly concerning the Church. In effect, truth forms consciences and directs efforts to promote unity.

36 With regard to the study of areas of disagreement, the Council requires that the whole body of doctrine be clearly presented. At the same time, . . . the manner and method of expounding the Catholic faith should not be a hindrance to dialogue with our brothers and sisters.

These passages suggest an act of imagination. The truth at the heart of the new evangelization challenges us to imagine in hope a future situation in which our differences no longer divide us. This situation must not be one where, under the pressures of doctrinal minimalism, we will have accepted a pluralism of positions that cannot be harmonized. On the contrary, embracing an authentic catholicity, the entire "content of revealed truth" should be affirmed as it was before our differences divided us, but in a way that encompasses a range of differences that no longer divide us. *Ut Unum Sint* invites us to do just this: "What is needed is a calm, clear-sighted and truthful vision of things, a vision enlivened by divine mercy and capable of freeing people's minds and inspiring in everyone a renewed willingness, precisely with a view to proclaiming the gospel to men and women of every people and nation" (*UUS*, §2).

The encyclical urges us to receive the results that the dialogues have produced to date (*UUS*, §80). They have achieved a tremendous amount: clearing away negative perceptions, drawing our attention to convergences that had never been recognized, and acknowledging the elements of authentic Christian faith in other Christian communities. "Elements of sanctification and truth present in the other Christian communities . . . constitute the objective basis of the communion, albeit imperfect, which exists between them and the Catholic Church" (*UUS*, §11).

The "unity bestowed by the Holy Spirit does not merely consist in the gathering of people as a collection of individuals" (*UUS*, §9). "It is not a matter of adding together all the riches scattered throughout the various Christian communities in order to arrive at a Church which God has in mind for the future. . . . In the Pentecost event, God has already manifested the Church in her eschatological reality. . . . This reality is something already given. . . . Ecumenism is directed precisely to making the partial communion existing between Christians grow towards full communion in truth and charity" (*UUS*, §14).

Suppose that we were to make operative the eschatological reality of the church, the full communion in truth and charity for which we long, in actual experiments in the new evangelization. Suppose that Lutherans and Catholics or Anglicans and Catholics attempted joint efforts in evangelization. What forms might such evangelization take, not just in terms of strategy but also in terms of proclaiming the gospel? Rather than thinking about how to resolve our doctrinal differences, let us ask ourselves what gospel we would preach if we applied a maximalist rather than a minimalist standard of the full content of revealed truth. The evangelical challenge to renewed ecumenical commitment is that we would understand our goal to be the affirmation of the entire content of revealed truth encompassing a wide range of formulations. Under this understanding, dogmas are intended to permit as many — not as few — expressions as are compatible with the truth in matters of faith and morals, "precisely with a view to proclaiming the gospel to men and women of every people and nation" (*UUS*, §2).

Someone said to me today that he hoped that, since this was to be a banquet address, I would make you laugh. If I have not moved you to laughter, I hope that I have stirred you to renewed zeal both for the ecumenical venture and for the new evangelization. For it is clear that they cannot be separated.

"Believers in Christ . . . cannot remain divided. If they wish truly and effectively to oppose the world's tendency to reduce to powerlessness the mystery of redemption, they must profess together the same truth about the cross . . . of Jesus, the one redeemer of man" (*UUS*, §1,2).

Thank you.